MAIN LIBRARY

ACPL

S0-ATI-498

DISCARDED

332.152 G61e 2296483
Goode, Richard B.
Economic assistance to
developing countries...

DO NOT REMOVE
CARDS FROM POCKET

ALLEN COUNTY PUBLIC LIBRARY

FORT WAYNE, INDIANA 46802

You may return this book to any agency, branch,
or bookmobile of the Allen County Public Library.

DEMCO

*Studies in International Economics*

# Economic Assistance to Developing Countries Through the IMF

*Richard Goode*

THE BROOKINGS INSTITUTION
*Washington, D.C.*

*© 1985 by*

THE BROOKINGS INSTITUTION

*1775 Massachusetts Avenue, N.W., Washington, D.C. 20036*

*Library of Congress Catalog Card Number 85-072319*
*ISBN 0-8157-3193-0*

9 8 7 6 5 4 3 2 1

Allen County Public Library
Ft. Wayne, Indiana

2296483

*Board of Trustees*
Robert V. Roosa
*Chairman*
Louis W. Cabot
*Vice Chairman;*
*Chairman, Executive Committee*
Ralph S. Saul
*Vice Chairman;*
*Chairman, Development Committee*
Samuel H. Armacost
J. David Barnes
Rex J. Bates
Frank T. Cary
A. W. Clausen
William T. Coleman, Jr.
Lloyd N. Cutler
Thomas R. Donahue
Charles W. Duncan, Jr.
Walter Y. Elisha
Robert F. Erburu
Hanna H. Gray
Robert D. Haas
Philip M. Hawley
Amory Houghton, Jr.
Roy M. Huffington
B. R. Inman
James T. Lynn
Donald F. McHenry
Bruce K. MacLaury
Robert S. McNamara
Mary Patterson McPherson
Donald S. Perkins
J. Woodward Redmond
Charles W. Robinson
James D. Robinson III
Henry B. Schacht
Roger D. Semerad
Howard R. Swearer
Morris Tanenbaum
Phyllis A. Wallace
James D. Wolfensohn
Ezra K. Zilkha
Charles J. Zwick

*Honorary Trustees*
Vincent M. Barnett, Jr.
Barton M. Biggs
Eugene R. Black
Robert D. Calkins
Edward W. Carter
Bruce B. Dayton
Douglas Dillon
George M. Elsey
Huntington Harris
Andrew Heiskell
Roger W. Heyns
John E. Lockwood
William McC. Martin, Jr.
Arjay Miller
Charles W. Robinson
H. Chapman Rose
Gerard C. Smith
Robert Brookings Smith
Sydney Stein, Jr.

THE BROOKINGS INSTITUTION is an independent organization devoted to nonpartisan research, education, and publication in economics, government, foreign policy, and the social sciences generally. Its principal purposes are to aid in the development of sound public policies and to promote public understanding of issues of national importance.

The Institution was founded on December 8, 1927, to merge the activities of the Institute for Government Research, founded in 1916, the Institute of Economics, founded in 1922, and the Robert Brookings Graduate School of Economics and Government, founded in 1924.

The Board of Trustees is responsible for the general administration of the Institution, while the immediate direction of the policies, program, and staff is vested in the President, assisted by an advisory committee of the officers and staff. The by-laws of the Institution state: "It is the function of the Trustees to make possible the conduct of scientific research, and publication, under the most favorable conditions, and to safeguard the independence of the research staff in the pursuit of their studies and in the publication of the results of such studies. It is not a part of their function to determine, control, or influence the conduct of particular investigations or the conclusions reached."

The President bears final responsibility for the decision to publish a manuscript as a Brookings book. In reaching his judgment on the competence, accuracy, and objectivity of each study, the President is advised by the director of the appropriate research program and weighs the views of a panel of expert outside readers who report to him in confidence on the quality of the work. Publication of a work signifies that it is deemed a competent treatment worthy of public consideration but does not imply endorsement of conclusions or recommendations.

The Institution maintains its position of neutrality on issues of public policy in order to safeguard the intellectual freedom of the staff. Hence interpretations or conclusions in Brookings publications should be understood to be solely those of the authors and should not be attributed to the Institution, to its trustees, officers, or other staff members, or to the organizations that support its research.

# *Foreword*

THE MEMBERSHIP and scope of the activities of the International Monetary Fund have expanded greatly since it began operations in 1946. In support of its primary purposes of promoting international monetary cooperation, orderly exchange arrangements, and balance-of-payments adjustment, the IMF has extended substantial amounts of credit to member countries and has allocated special drawing rights to them. Developing countries have especially benefited from the IMF's basic financing and from certain facilities designed mainly for them.

In this study Richard Goode describes IMF policies and operations and examines the question whether the IMF, besides discharging its other functions, should provide additional economic assistance to developing countries. He analyzes the possible advantages and disadvantages of alternative proposals and discusses the relation between the IMF and the World Bank. He emphasizes that the function of serving as a channel for economic assistance to developing countries should be considered as distinctly secondary to the IMF's other activities.

Richard Goode is a guest scholar at the Brookings Institution. He is indebted to Ralph C. Bryant and Sir Joseph Gold for advice and for critical reading of an early draft of the study. He also acknowledges with thanks comments and suggestions from W. A. Beveridge, Sidney Dell, Barend de Vries, Margaret Garritsen de Vries, C. David Finch, Edward R. Fried, Walter Habermeier, Leslie Lipschitz, Richard P. Mattione, Costas Michalopoulos, Walter S. Salant, Robert Solomon, Alan A. Tait, C. A. Yandle, and several participants in a workshop on the evolution of the International Monetary Fund held at Brookings on January 7, 1985. Carol Clark edited the manuscript, Carolyn A. Rutsch verified its factual content, and Charlotte Kaiser did the typing.

This study was supported by an experimental grant in international economic policy awarded to the Brookings Institution by the National Science Foundation. The views expressed here are those of the author and should not be ascribed to those who commented on the manuscript, to the National Science Foundation, or to the officers, trustees, or staff members of the Brookings Institution.

BRUCE K. MAC LAURY
*President*

*July 1985*
*Washington, D.C.*

THE FORTY-FIVE countries that took part in the Bretton Woods Conference in 1944 agreed to establish the International Monetary Fund (IMF) to promote international monetary cooperation and to facilitate international trade, thereby contributing to the maintenance of high levels of employment and real income and the development of productive resources. More specifically, the IMF was intended to promote exchange stability and orderly exchange arrangements and to assist in eliminating foreign exchange restrictions. It was expected to make its resources "temporarily available" to members "under adequate safeguards, thus providing them with opportunity to correct maladjustments in their balance of payments without resorting to measures destructive of national or international prosperity."[1]

Although the Articles of Agreement of the IMF have been amended twice (effective in 1969 and 1978), the original statement of purposes remains unaltered. During the last forty years, however, the membership has grown to 148 countries, and important changes have occurred in the IMF's operations and policies. The institution survived the breakdown in the early 1970s of the par value system of relatively fixed exchange rates, which had been widely regarded as an essential feature of the IMF. It was authorized to issue special drawing rights (SDRs) as a supplement to other international reserve assets, but the allocations have been smaller and less regular than expected. Consultations with members have become a major function, and the IMF has been enjoined to exercise surveillance over exchange rate policies of members and international liquidity.

After early disagreements, IMF lending policies have been worked out and adapted over the years. Initially, financial assistance was provided in only one way; charges were uniform for members but were graduated according to complex schedules. In time, special needs of groups of members—particularly developing countries—were recognized by the establishment of several special policies or facilities for the use of the Fund's financial resources. Larger drawings in relation to quotas were permitted. Charges were simplified and, to a limited extent, subsidized for low-income countries. Longer periods of continuous use of Fund credit were

1. Articles of Agreement of the International Monetary Fund, Article I, as amended to 1978.

allowed. Resources were augmented by periodic quota increases and by borrowing. These developments were approved by the executive board and, in some cases, by votes of the governors and member governments, but they were disturbing to some, while others thought they did not go far enough.

This study examines the question whether the IMF, in addition to its other functions, should assume a larger role in providing economic assistance to developing countries. Economic assistance is interpreted as the transfer of resources on more favorable terms and in larger amounts than would flow from commercial lending and private direct investment.

The subject of additional economic assistance to the developing countries is timely because of the adverse impact on them of the recent worldwide recession, the prospect that some of the poorest countries will not participate fully in the recovery, the unfavorable terms of trade of the non-oil developing countries, the persistent external debt problem, and the expectation that per capita income will continue to stagnate or decline in some countries. External assistance can encourage and complement policies that will help developing countries strengthen their balance of payments and domestic economies, resulting in beneficial effects on world trade and finance.

The provision of additional economic assistance through the IMF would be an extension of past practices rather than a new departure. All users of the Fund's financial resources have been assisted. Developing countries have received especially significant amounts of economic assistance because they have drawn on the Fund's basic financing and special facilities to a much greater extent than have the industrial countries. In addition, part of the Fund's gold has been used for the benefit of the developing countries.

The study first reviews the evolution of attitudes toward the Fund's functions and its concern with developing countries. Next, the history of Fund financial operations is summarized. The relationship between the IMF and the World Bank is then described, and the tendency is noted for each institution to concern itself more with matters that previously were considered the responsibility of the other. In addition to larger credits on normal terms, four possible forms of economic assistance to developing countries are examined. These are a subsidy for IMF charges payable by low-income countries, a soft-loan window at the IMF analogous to the International Development Association affiliate of the World Bank, a link between special drawing rights and aid or development finance, and a facility to provide external debt relief. A final section presents some conclusions on the merits of the proposals and mentions considerations that might persuade the international community to channel additional economic assistance to developing countries through the IMF instead of relying entirely on bilateral programs, the World Bank group, or another international organization. It also addresses the question whether the provision of additional economic assistance through the IMF would detract from its other functions or would damage its status as an international monetary institution.

## Evolution of the IMF's Policies

The preparatory work and the discussion of plans for the IMF at the Bretton Woods Conference concerned mainly the problems of the industrial countries. A proposal by India that the Fund give special attention to "the fuller utilization of the resources of economically underdeveloped countries" was rejected in favor of language in the Articles of Agreement referring to "the development of the productive resources of all members as [one of the] primary objectives of economic policy."[2]

In the Bretton Woods Agreement Act, which authorized U.S. membership in the Fund, the U.S. Congress required the U.S. governor and executive director to obtain an official interpretation by the Fund "as to whether its authority to use its resources extends beyond current monetary stabilization operations to afford temporary assistance to members in connection with seasonal, cyclical, and emergency fluctuations in the balance of payments . . . for current transactions, and whether it has authority to use its resources to provide facilities for relief, reconstruction, or armaments, or to meet a large or sustained outflow of capital. . . ." Soon after the beginning of Fund operations in 1946, the executive directors gave the requested interpretation, holding that the "authority to use the resources of the Fund is limited to use in accordance with its purposes to give temporary assistance in financing balance of payments deficits on current account for monetary stabilization operations." In 1961 this interpretation was clarified by a decision stating that it did not preclude the use of the Fund's resources for capital transfers "in accordance with the . . . Articles."[3]

2. J. Keith Horsefield, *The International Monetary Fund, 1945–1965: Twenty Years of International Monetary Cooperation*, vol. 1: *Chronicle* (IMF, 1969), pp. 85, 93–94.

3. Ibid., pp. 115, 149, 506.

*Basic Financing*

IMF financing takes the form of purchases or drawings of needed foreign currencies in exchange for the member's currency. Drawings in the reserve tranche, which merely return to the member resources it has provided, are readily available. (The reserve tranche results from the member's payment of a portion of its quota in prescribed foreign currencies or special drawing rights, drawings of its currency by other members, and certain other movements in the IMF's holdings of its currency.) Further drawings are in the credit tranches and are normally subject to conditions mentioned in the next paragraph. Credit tranche drawings are normally subject to a limit equal to 100 percent of the member's quota, but the Fund can make and has made exceptions to increase the limit. Although credit tranche drawings are not loans in the legal sense, they are economically equivalent to loans and are generally called Fund credits. Fund credit is for balance of payments support rather than for development projects, and IMF basic financing is not tied to specific imports or foreign payments.[4]

After some early controversy, the Fund decided in 1948 that the use of its resources was not an unchallengeable right of members but was subject to prior approval. A policy on conditions for the use of Fund credit was adopted in 1952. It has been restated and elaborated from time to time, most recently in a 1979 executive board decision.[5] The conditions are more severe for the upper credit tranches (the second, third, and fourth of four tranches, each of which is equivalent to 25 percent of the member's quota) than for the first credit tranche.

Credit is usually extended under a standby arrangement, which assures a member that it may draw on the Fund up to a specified amount in a given period without further review of its policies, provided it has observed the conditions and other terms of the arrangement. If the conditions—particularly those designated as performance criteria—are not observed, the member's access to further drawings is interrupted. Standby arrangements traditionally have allowed drawings during a one-year period, and members have been expected to repay Fund credit within three to five years, or earlier if their balance of payments allows.

4. A brief description of the IMF and its methods of operation and facilities can be found in A. W. Hooke, *The International Monetary Fund: Its Evolution, Organization, and Activities*, IMF Pamphlet Series 37, 3d ed. (IMF, 1983). See also Joseph Gold, *Financial Assistance by the International Monetary Fund: Law and Practice*, IMF Pamphlet Series 27, 2d ed. (IMF, 1980); Anand G. Chandarvarkar, *The International Monetary Fund: Its Financial Organization and Activities*, IMF Pamphlet Series 42 (IMF, 1984).

5. International Monetary Fund, *Annual Report of the Executive Board for the Financial Year Ended April 30, 1979*, pp. 136–38. Hereafter IMF, *Annual Report, 19–*.

The conditions for use of the Fund's resources are intended to ensure the attainment of a viable balance of payments without resorting to harmful direct controls and to enable the member to terminate its use of Fund credit within a reasonable period. The 1979 board decision on access to Fund credit states, "In helping members to devise adjustment programs, the Fund will pay due regard to the domestic social and political objectives, the economic priorities, and the circumstances of members, including the causes of their balance of payments problems." The decision further provides that performance criteria may vary from case to case but will be limited to those "necessary to evaluate implementation of the program." Performance criteria "will normally be confined to (i) macroeconomic variables, and (ii) those necessary to implement specific provisions of the Articles [of Agreement] or policies adopted under them." Other performance criteria may be adopted only "in exceptional cases when . . . essential for the effectiveness of the member's program because of their macroeconomic impact."[6]

Over time the size of members' drawings permitted in relation to quota has increased substantially. The original Articles of Agreement limited a member's drawings in any one year to 25 percent of its quota unless the Fund granted a waiver.[7] No waiver was granted until 1953. During the first five years of operations, 68 percent of all drawings fell in what would now be called the reserve tranche and 32 percent in the first credit tranche. After the mid-1950s, waivers became more common and finally more or less routine in connection with standby arrangements.[8] The annual limit on drawings was eliminated by the second amendment.

### *Special Facilities*

The original view of the IMF as an institution that treats all members uniformly and that provides only temporary balance of payments finance, distinct from other capital-account transactions (for example, lending or aid intended to promote economic development), greatly influenced its history and remains the dominant official view. Over the years, however, the interpretation of these principles has gradually evolved. In particular, the Articles of Agreement were interpreted to allow the establishment of

6. Ibid.

7. Technically, the limit applied to drawings that would raise the Fund's holdings of the member's currency by more than 25 percent of its quota, but only to the extent that the Fund's holdings were brought above 75 percent of quota.

8. Margaret G. de Vries and J. Keith Horsefield, *The International Monetary Fund, 1945–1965: Twenty Years of International Monetary Cooperation,* vol. 2: *Analysis* (IMF, 1969), pp. 403, 406.

policies or facilities to meet special balance of payments problems associated with the needs of particular classes of members and also to permit lengthening the period of continuous use of IMF financial resources and providing explicit subsidies for poor countries.

*General Arrangements to Borrow.* The first special facility in the IMF, the General Arrangements to Borrow (GAB), established in 1962, provided a means of financing a particular kind of transaction rather than a policy on the use of Fund credit. The GAB provided for lending to the Fund by ten major industrial countries or their central banks (the United States, the United Kingdom, West Germany, France, Italy, Japan, Canada, the Netherlands, Belgium, and Sweden—later known as the Group of Ten) when required to finance drawings by the participating countries. The IMF concluded a parallel agreement with the Swiss National Bank. The GAB was to be activated only "to forestall or cope with an impairment of the international monetary system."[9] GAB countries were not given larger drawing rights, but the special character and magnitude of their possible needs were recognized.

The GAB was revised and enlarged in late 1983 to allow Fund borrowing to finance lending to member countries that are not GAB participants under exceptional conditions that threaten the stability of the international monetary system. In early 1984, Switzerland became a full participant.[10]

*Compensatory financing facility.* In 1963, in response to extensive discussions in the United Nations and the Organization of American States, the compensatory financing facility was created principally to assist primary producing countries. The Fund announced that it was prepared to provide financing to members suffering an export shortfall of a "short-term character . . . largely attributable to circumstances beyond the control of the member." The usual conditionality standards were not to be applied, provided the member undertook to cooperate with the Fund, if required, to find appropriate solutions to its balance of payments difficulties. The normal limitation on drawings in relation to quota would be waived when necessary, and the Fund invited countries whose quotas were inadequate in the light of export fluctuations to apply for increases.[11]

9. Horsefield, *The International Monetary Fund, 1945–1965,* vol. 1, pp. 507–16.

10. IMF, *Annual Report, 1983*, pp. 94–95; IMF, *Annual Report, 1984*, pp. 81–82; Michael Ainley, *The General Arrangements to Borrow*, IMF Pamphlet Series 41 (IMF, 1984).

11. Horsefield, *The International Monetary Fund, 1945–65*, vol. 1, pp. 531–36; J. Keith Horsefield and Gertrud Lovasy, "Evolution of the Fund's Policy on Drawings," in de Vries and Horsefield, *The International Monetary Fund, 1945–65,* vol. 2, pp. 417–27; Louis M. Goreux, *Compensatory Financing Facility*, IMF Pamphlet Series 34 (IMF, 1980).

The compensatory financing facility was later modified to expand access and to require for large drawings in relation to quota that the Fund be satisfied that the member is, in fact, cooperating to find solutions to its balance of payments difficulties.[12] Guidelines approved by the executive board in 1983 interpret the requirement of cooperation with the Fund for an upper credit tranche drawing under the compensatory financing facility as equivalent to meeting the usual conditionality standards for an upper credit tranche program.[13]

The facility was regarded as consistent with the principle of uniformity because it was available to all members suffering from the particular balance of payments problem to which it was addressed. As stated by the IMF's former general counsel:

> The legal justification for a special policy is that there is a balance of payments difficulty that can be distinguished from other difficulties according to bona fide economic criteria, and that there are good reasons consistent with the Fund's purposes why the particular difficulty should be the subject of a special policy on use of the Fund's resources. The policy must then have an intrinsic relationship to the difficulty for which it was designed.[14]

This line of reasoning was highly influential in the development of additional special policies and facilities.

*Buffer stock financing facility.* Established in 1969, the buffer stock financing facility was, in the words of the IMF's official history, "the Fund's answer to the demands of the developing countries . . . that the Fund and the World Bank pay greater heed to the problem of stabilization of prices of primary products."[15] This facility provided for IMF financing to help members make their contributions to an international buffer stock. Like the initial compensatory financing facility, the buffer stock financing facility required only mild conditionality, and the usual limits on drawings were not applicable.[16] Except for Australia, only developing countries have used the facility.

*Oil facilities and subsidy.* In response to a sharp increase in oil prices, the IMF established a special oil facility in 1974 and a second oil facility in 1975. These facilities waived the usual quantitative limitations on

12. IMF, *Annual Report, 1982*, p. 80.

13. The member must either have in place an upper credit tranche arrangement in which its performance is "broadly satisfactory" or its current and prospective policies must meet the criteria for use of Fund resources in the upper credit tranches. See IMF, *Annual Report, 1984*, p. 137.

14. Gold, *Financial Assistance*, p. 29.

15. Margaret Garritsen de Vries, *The International Monetary Fund, 1966–1971*, vol. 1: *Narrative* (IMF, 1976), p. 269.

16. Ibid., pp. 269–81.

drawings. For the 1974 facility, conditionality was minimal, but for the 1975 facility, users were required to describe their medium-term policies to deal with their balance of payments problems and to conserve oil or develop alternative energy sources, and the Fund had to assess the adequacy of the policies. Transactions were financed exclusively by Fund borrowing from sixteen member countries (including several of the major oil exporters) and Switzerland. Charges were related to the Fund's interest cost.[17]

Both industrial countries and developing countries used the oil facilities. However, in August 1975 special provision was made for developing countries by establishing an oil facility subsidy account to help those members most seriously affected by the rise in oil prices to meet the interest costs of using the 1975 oil facility. It was financed by voluntary contributions.[18]

*Extended Fund facility.* An important step in the evolution of Fund policies was the establishment in 1974 of the extended Fund facility. Recognizing that some countries needed more time to solve their balance of payments problems than had been contemplated in Fund programs (which usually covered one year with repayments of drawings expected within three to five years), the Fund decided that it would be willing to approve arrangements for periods up to three years with repayments to be completed within eight years (later extended to ten years). Drawings could exceed the normal quantitative limits. Access to the extended facility, as to basic financing, was made conditional on the Fund's appraisal of the adequacy of the member's policies. The policies were to be set out in a broad program for the entire period (up to three years) and in detailed programs for each year to be formulated before the beginning of the year. Drawings were to be phased over the period and, hence, would be subject to interruption if the performance conditions were not observed.

The facility was intended for members with "an economy suffering serious payments imbalance relating to structural maladjustments in production and trade and where prices and cost distortions have been widespread" or "an economy characterized by slow growth and an inherently weak balance of payments position which prevents pursuit of an active development policy."[19] Although only the second condition tied the facility explicitly to the needs of developing countries, in practice only those countries have used it.

17. IMF, *Annual Report, 1974*, pp. 52–53; IMF, *Annual Report, 1975*, pp. 53–54.
18. IMF, *Annual Report, 1976*, pp. 58–60.
19. IMF, *Annual Report, 1975*, pp. 54–55, 88–90; IMF, *Annual Report, 1981*, p. 84.

*Supplementary financing facility, enlarged access policy, and subsidy.* The supplementary financing facility was established in August 1977 and became operational in February 1979. It was intended to enable the Fund to make available greater than normal amounts of financing to members facing serious payments imbalances that were large in relation to their economies and their Fund quotas. The usual conditionality applied. The operations were financed by Fund borrowing from member countries and the Swiss National Bank, and charges for use were related to the Fund's costs plus a small margin.[20] Use of the borrowed resources of the supplementary financing facility and use of the Fund's ordinary resources were combined according to a formula.

The supplementary financing facility was replaced by a policy, adopted in 1981, providing for enlarged access to the Fund's resources. This facility was financed by medium-term borrowing from the Saudi Arabian Monetary Authority and from eighteen countries through the Bank for International Settlements. The borrowing costs were reflected in charges to members. Assistance generally could be provided up to 150 percent of the member's quota under a one-year standby arrangement and 450 percent of quota under a three-year arrangement, excluding transactions under the compensatory financing facility and the buffer stock facility. A member's cumulative access to Fund resources (net of the excluded facilities) could reach 600 percent of its quota.

The enlarged access policy was a transitional arrangement, pending an increase in Fund quotas. It was continued with modifications when the larger quotas provided by the eighth review of quotas came into effect on November 30, 1983 (discussed later).[21] Although not limited to developing countries, the supplementary financing facility and the enlarged access policy have been used only by them. In December 1980 a subsidy account was established to help low-income member countries meet the market-related cost of using the supplementary financing facility. The Fund operates the account as trustee.[22] No subsidy has been provided in connection with the enlarged access policy.

*Cereal imports facility.* In 1981 the Fund added to its compensatory financing facility for export shortfalls a facility for financing temporary increases in the cost of cereal imports resulting from conditions largely beyond the member's control. This facility is coordinated with the compensatory financing facility for exports and is not subject to normal con-

20. IMF, *Annual Report, 1978*, pp. 67–68, 112–15; IMF, *Annual Report, 1979*, pp. 74–75.
21. IMF, *Annual Report, 1984*, pp. 78, 130–35.
22. IMF, *Annual Report, 1981*, pp. 105–06.

ditionality standards.[23] Although not formally so restricted, the cereal imports facility is obviously intended only for developing countries.

*Disposal of Gold and Establishment of Trust Fund*

In the discussions of international monetary reform during the early 1970s that preceded the second amendment to the IMF's Articles of Agreement, it was agreed that the important role that gold had played in the Fund would be ended and special drawing rights would be made the unit of account and, at least formally, the principal reserve asset of the international monetary system. Fifty million ounces of gold, about one-third of the Fund's holdings, would be disposed of—25 million ounces to be distributed to members in proportion to their quotas and 25 million ounces to be sold for the benefit of less developed member countries. Since gold was selling at prices far above its official value, recipients of gold obtained a potential capital gain, and sales of gold yielded large profits.

The decision to use 25 million ounces of gold for the special benefit of less developed countries can be regarded as a weak substitute for the proposals for a link between SDRs and aid, which the developing countries had unsuccessfully urged (discussed in a later section). The 104 members classified as less developed countries received by direct transfer 27.8 percent of the profits from the sale of that gold, a share equal to their share of total Fund quotas. The remaining 72.2 percent of the profits was placed in a trust fund, to be administered by the IMF to finance balance of payments loans to the poorest member countries. To be eligible for trust fund loans in the two years from July 1976 through June 1978, a member had to have per capita income not in excess of SDR 300 in 1973; during the next two years the criterion was per capita income not in excess of SDR 520 in 1975. In addition, the country was required to have a need for balance of payments assistance and to be making a reasonable effort to strengthen its balance of payments. Forty-three countries qualified from 1976 to 1978 and fifty-three countries from 1978 to 1980.[24]

The less developed countries with relatively high incomes shared in the direct transfers of profits in proportion to quotas but not in the loans. However, some of the recipients returned all or part of their shares of the direct transfers of profits.[25]

23. Ibid., pp. 84–85.

24. Hooke, *International Monetary Fund,* p. 55.

25. Iraq, Kuwait, Qatar, Saudi Arabia, the United Arab Emirates, and Venezuela transferred the full amount of their profit shares back to the trust fund; Libya and Yugoslavia returned part of their shares, and Romania agreed to lend part of its share to the trust fund.

The trust fund loans were made at the low concessional interest rate of 0.5 percent and were made repayable in installments over the sixth to tenth years after their disbursement.[26]

### *Comments*

The record shows that the Fund has flexibly adapted its credit policies to changing perceptions of needs and its role. Members' access to Fund credit has been greatly expanded in relation to quotas through both the liberalization of basic financing and the addition of special facilities.

Three special facilities that continue in effect—the compensatory financing facility, the cereal imports facility, and the buffer stock financing facility—were designed mainly to serve financing needs of developing countries attributable to fluctuations in the prices and production of primary products. Because these needs were considered both temporary and largely beyond the member's control, the use of the facilities was initially subject to low conditionality, and it did not reduce the member's access to the Fund's basic financing.

Some persons argued that the special facilities were unnecessary because the needs could have been met by a flexible application of policies governing access to the Fund's regular financing. That position seems unrealistic because it minimizes the difficulties that would have been encountered in the more discretionary application of the usual guidelines for basic financing, and neglects the political advantages of responding concretely to insistent recommendations from other international organizations and unofficial sources. The recent decision to apply essentially the same degree of conditionality for the compensatory financing facility as for regular drawings, however, may diminish its special character and weaken the case for its continuance.

By establishing the extended Fund facility in 1974, the IMF conceded that the balance of payments deficits of some developing countries were less amenable to quick correction than previously had been assumed. To be sure, successive standby arrangements had been approved for a number of countries, but limiting most of the arrangements to one year seemed to imply an unrealistic view of the duration of the problem in many cases and to bias the choice of corrective measures toward demand reduction. In practice, however, the extended facility has been used less

26. On the trust fund, see IMF, *Annual Report, 1976*, p. 60; IMF, *Annual Report, 1978*, pp. 76–79; IMF, *Annual Report, 1980*, pp. 85–89; IMF, *Annual Report, 1981*, p. 104.

frequently than might have been expected. During the first five years after the facility was established, only eleven extended arrangements were approved (of which two were with Jamaica).[27] At the end of 1984 there were outstanding twenty-nine standby arrangements and only four extended arrangements (with Brazil, the Dominican Republic, Malawi, and Mexico).[28]

The supplementary financing facility and the enlarged access policy were adopted to allow members with serious problems, especially developing countries, to obtain larger amounts of credit than would have been available according to normal guidelines. Operating these facilities apparently was considered more feasible than ad hoc exceptions to the normal guidelines. Possibly more important was the fact that the facilities were financed by Fund borrowing and, hence, did not divert resources from other uses. The facilities were especially useful during the troubled periods before the increases in quotas that became effective in 1980 and 1983. The enlarged access policy remains in operation in modified form.

The two oil facilities, the distribution of profits from gold sales, and the trust fund loans are of historical interest and may have some significance for the future. The creation of the oil facilities, which served both industrial countries and developing countries, was an example of exceptionally quick action to respond to a massive, unprecedented problem. Whether in retrospect the approach was as desirable as it seemed at the time could be debated, but such a discussion will not be undertaken here. Nor is it necessary, for present purposes, to evaluate the political compromise embodied in the distribution of profits from gold sales and the trust fund. The gold sales, however, offer a precedent for possible further use of IMF gold to finance assistance to developing countries.

## IMF Financial Operations, 1947–84

Member countries obtain economic resources by using IMF credit. As explained earlier, the transactions are, in effect, loans that must be repaid within three to five years or, in some cases, ten years. To the extent that Fund charges are lower than market interest rates, the use of Fund credit

27. IMF, *International Financial Statistics: Supplement on Fund Accounts,* no. 3 (1982), p. 148.

28. Fourteen of the standby arrangements covered a period longer than the traditional twelve months; in one case the period was two years. See *IMF Survey*, February 4, 1985, p. 46.

involves an implicit subsidy. For some uses, explicit subsidies have been provided.

### *Use of Fund Credit*

Developing countries have used Fund credit to a much greater extent than industrial countries in absolute amounts and especially in relation to IMF quotas (see table 1). From 1947 through 1984 the cumulative (gross) use of Fund credit by non-oil developing countries equaled 232 percent of their quotas at the end of the period, compared with 28 percent for industrial countries and only 8 percent for oil-exporting developing countries. Almost 65 percent of the use of Fund credit by the non-oil developing countries was obtained through facilities that especially serve their needs—the compensatory financing facility for export shortfalls, the cereal imports facility, the buffer stock financing facility, the supplementary financing facility and the enlarged access policy, and the extended Fund facility.

Table 1. *IMF Quotas and Cumulative Use of Fund Credit, by Groups of Countries, as of December 31, 1984*[a]
Millions of SDRs

| | | | *Developing countries* | |
|---|---|---|---|---|
| *Item* | *All members* | *Industrial countries* | *Oil exporters* | *Non-oil countries* |
| Quotas | 89,302 | 56,089 | 9,752 | 23,461 |
| Use of Fund credit[a] | 71,154 | 15,979 | 764 | 54,372 |
| Ordinary transactions[b] | 27,641 | 11,778 | 314 | 15,510 |
| Supplementary financing facility and enlarged access policy | 9,139 | 0 | 0 | 9,139 |
| Extended facility | | | | |
| Ordinary resources | 6,923 | 0 | 0 | 6,923 |
| Borrowed resources | 6,565 | 0 | 0 | 6,565 |
| Compensatory financing[c] | 13,425 | 653 | 378 | 12,395 |
| Buffer stock financing facility | 558 | 56 | 72 | 429 |
| Oil facilities | 6,903 | 3,492 | 0 | 3,411 |

Source: International Monetary Fund, *International Financial Statistics,* February 1985, pp. 20–22.

a. Fund credit is defined as all drawings other than reserve tranche drawings. The amounts shown are gross drawings (without deduction of repayments) cumulated from 1947, when the first drawings occurred, to the end of 1984.

b. Details for country groups will not add to the total for all members because the total, but not the details, includes use by countries that are no longer members.

c. Compensatory financing facility for export shortfalls and the cereal imports facility.

Gradually, there has been a great change in the distribution of use of Fund credit among groups of member countries. During the first twenty-seven years of lending operations, 1947–73, drawings by industrial countries accounted for 54 percent of total Fund credit and drawings by all developing countries accounted for 46 percent. In the period 1974–84 the share of the industrial countries fell to 14 percent, while that of the non-oil developing countries rose to 85 percent, and that of the oil-exporting developing countries was less than 1 percent.[29] After 1977, no industrial country made an ordinary credit tranche drawing.

The breakdown of the par value system in 1973 probably was a cause of the diminished relative use of Fund credit by industrial countries in later years. Although not indifferent to their exchange rates, the industrial countries (notably the United Kingdom) felt less need to use Fund credit to defend them after 1973.[30] Other factors may have been the ready availability of credit from banks and other lenders and the reluctance of the industrial countries to accept the conditionality required by the Fund. The public attention and political controversy provoked by discussions concerning the applications for standby arrangements by the United Kingdom in 1976 and by Italy in 1974 and 1977 may have discouraged further recourse to the IMF by the governments of industrial countries. Conceivably, an impression that the Fund was becoming an institution for lending to less developed countries rather than a source of temporary balance of payments finance for all members was a deterrent to industrial countries, but confirmation or refutation of that conjecture may have to await the publication and critical review of the memoirs of leading politicians and central bankers.

Although a large portion of drawings on the IMF had been repaid, the non-oil developing countries had outstanding Fund credits of SDR 34.5 billion—147 percent of their quotas—as of December 31, 1984.[31] Undrawn balances under outstanding standby arrangements and extended arrangements at that date totaled SDR 6.6 billion, equal to 28 percent of

29. Total purchases less reserve tranche drawings. IMF, *International Financial Statistics: Supplement on Fund Accounts,* no. 3 (1982), pp. 10–15; IMF, *International Financial Statistics,* February 1985, pp. 20–22.

30. In 1978–83 France and Italy, which had previously borrowed from the Fund, ran substantial cumulative deficits in their current accounts, while the United Kingdom, another earlier borrower, realized a substantial cumulative current account surplus. Over the period as a whole, the nominal exchange rates of all three countries depreciated considerably. The smaller industrial countries as a group ran substantial current account deficits in each of the years from 1978 through 1983. See International Monetary Fund, *World Economic Outlook,* IMF Occasional Paper 27 (IMF, 1984), pp. 188, 214, 216, 217.

31. IMF, *International Financial Statistics*, February 1985, p. 32.

the quotas of these countries. At the end of 1984 only one industrial country (Iceland) and one oil-exporting country (Indonesia) were using Fund credit; in both cases the credit reflected a purchase under the compensatory financing facility, and the amount outstanding was small in relation to the member's quota.[32]

*Implicit Subsidization of Fund Credit from Ordinary Resources*

The schedule of charges for the use of IMF credit has varied over time. The charges include a one-time service charge on drawings beyond the reserve tranche and periodic charges on outstanding balances in the credit tranches. The service charge is 0.5 percent. For many years, the periodic charges were elaborately graduated according to the amount of use in relation to the member's quota and the duration of use. In 1981 the executive board decided that a single rate of charge for the use of ordinary resources should be applied. It would be fixed at the beginning of each financial year "on the basis of the estimated income and expense of the Fund for the year and the target amount of net income for the year."[33]

From May 1982 through April 1984 the periodic charge was 6.6 percent a year for transactions financed from the Fund's ordinary resources. Effective May 1, 1984, the rate was raised to 7.0 percent. These rates, like the rates charged in prior years, were well below market interest rates. For example, the London Interbank Offer Rate for three-month SDR deposits averaged 11.96 percent in 1982, 9.05 percent in 1983, and 9.29 percent in 1984.[34] In the past, the Fund staff had argued that charges should be lower than market interest rates to encourage members with balance of payments needs to use the Fund's resources, though not low enough to discourage repayments. Some executive directors for developing countries had asserted that, because the Fund was intended to help members, market interest rates had no relevance for its charges, but executive directors for industrial countries did not accept that position.[35]

The 6.6 percent and 7 percent rates of periodic charge were also well below the average rate of remuneration paid to members on creditor

32. Ibid., p. 32.

33. IMF, *Annual Report, 1981*, p. 93. The principal source of Fund income in addition to charges is interest on the general department's holdings of SDRs; the main items of expense are remuneration to members whose currencies are used, interest paid on borrowings, and administrative expense.

34. IMF, *International Financial Statistics*, March 1985, p. 62.

35. de Vries, *The International Monetary Fund, 1966–1971*, vol. 1, pp. 378–79.

balances—9.50 percent in 1982, 7.42 percent in 1983, and 7.78 percent in 1984.[36] The rate of remuneration can exceed the rate of periodic charge because the IMF receives income from sources other than periodic charges and because it pays no remuneration on a considerable part of the currencies it lends. Remuneration is paid only on the amount by which the Fund's holdings of a member's currency fall below a norm equal to 75 percent of the member's quota on April 1, 1978 (the effective date of the second amendment to the Articles of Agreement) plus subsequent increases in its quota.[37]

A low rate of periodic charge results in an implicit subsidy for the use of Fund credit. This is equivalent to a concessional or grant element in the credit. The grant element may be stated as the difference between the nominal amount of a loan and the discounted present value of the payments of interest and repayments of principal. In evaluating the grant element of official loans, future debt service payments are conventionally discounted at a 10 percent interest rate; however, discounting at a rate equal to the recipient's alternative borrowing cost or the return on real assets in the country would be justified.[38] Borrowing costs have been above 10 percent in recent years. In 1982–84 interest rates paid by developing countries on new loans from private creditors and the World Bank were in the range of 11 to 13 percent and, in addition, commitment charges and other fees were frequently applied. Rates on private credits were much higher in 1981.[39]

Calculated at the conventional discount rate of 10 percent, the combination of a 0.5 percent service charge and a 7.0 percent periodic charge results in a 9.6 percent grant element for a drawing that is repaid in three to five years in accordance with Fund policy for ordinary transactions.[40] At a more realistic discount rate of 12 percent, the grant element is 15.6 percent. For a drawing under an extended Fund arrangement financed from ordinary resources, the grant element is 40.8 percent with a 12 percent discount rate (repurchases assumed to be made in equal semiannual installments in the fifth to tenth years).

36. IMF, *International Financial Statistics*, March 1985, p. 62.

37. A special rule governs the remuneration computation for members joining the Fund after April 1, 1978.

38. Danny M. Leipziger, "Lending Versus Giving: The Economics of Foreign Assistance," *World Development*, vol. 11 (April 1983), pp. 329–35; Leipziger, "The Concessionality of Foreign Assistance," *Finance and Development*, March 1984, pp. 44–46.

39. World Bank, *World Debt Tables: External Debt of Developing Countries, 1984–85* (World Bank, 1985), pp. xiii, 3.

40. This calculation assumes that the service charge is paid at the time of the drawing, periodic charges are paid at the end of each quarter, and repurchases are made in eight equal quarterly installments during the fourth and fifth years after the drawing.

The periodic charge for the use of Fund credit may increase in relation to market interest rates in the future, owing to the policy adopted in 1981 and a later decision on the rate of remuneration that will tend to reduce the Fund's net income. In January 1984 the executive board decided to gradually raise the rate of remuneration in relation to the SDR interest rate.[41] The rate of remuneration was then 85 percent of the SDR interest rate; it was increased to at least 88.33 percent of the SDR interest rate effective May 1, 1984, and was scheduled to rise to at least 91.66 percent and 94.99 percent of the SDR interest rate on May 1, 1985, and May 1, 1986, respectively.[42]

### *Implicit and Explicit Subsidization of Fund Credit from Borrowed Resources*

A little more than one-third of the cumulative use of Fund credit by developing countries until the end of 1984 was financed from borrowed resources. (Included are drawings under the oil facilities, the supplementary financing facility, and the enlarged access policy and part of the drawings under the extended facility. See table 1.)

The concessional element is smaller in these transactions than in other drawings because users must pay market-related interest rates. There is, nevertheless, an implicit subsidy element for most developing countries because the interest rate is lower than that which they would have to pay on other loans. The rate of interest paid by the Fund—and passed on to members—for borrowing in connection with the supplementary financing facility and the enlarged access policy, is a floating rate related to the yield of either U.S. Treasury securities with a five-year maturity or a basket of five-year-maturity securities of the countries whose currencies compose the valuation basket for the SDR (see section on special drawing rights).[43]

*Oil facility subsidy.* The oil facility subsidy account was the first example of an explicit subsidy to help poor countries meet the cost of Fund credit. It was established in August 1975 to assist in meeting the interest costs of using the 1975 oil facility. Those members most seriously affected

41. *IMF Survey*, January 9, 1984, p. 1. The Articles Agreement provide that the rate of remuneration shall be fixed within the range of 80 percent to 100 percent of the SDR interest rate [Article V, sec. 9(a)].

42. IMF, *Annual Report, 1984*, pp. 129–30.

43. In the year ended April 30, 1984, the average interest rates paid by the Fund on outstanding borrowings were 11.49 percent for the supplementary financing facility and 10.32 percent for the enlarged access policy. IMF, *Annual Report, 1984,* pp. 84–85.

by the 1973–74 rise in oil prices were eligible for the subsidy. Financed by contributions of twenty-five countries (including Switzerland, a nonmember, but not including the United States), subsidy payments to twenty-five beneficiaries amounted to a cumulative total of SDR 187 million by August 1983, after the final repurchases under the oil facility were scheduled and the account was terminated. The subsidy payments equaled 69 percent of the total charges paid by the beneficiaries on their drawings under the facility and provided a grant element of 30 percent for those drawings.[44]

*Subsidy for supplementary financing facility.* The supplementary financing facility subsidy account, as previously mentioned, was established in 1980 to reduce the cost for low-income developing countries of drawings under the supplementary financing facility. Eligibility for subsidies depends on per capita income. Member countries with per capita income in 1979 equal to or below that used to determine eligibility for assistance from the World Bank affiliate, the International Development Association (IDA), receive the full rate of subsidy, which does not exceed 3 percent a year; those with per capita income in 1979 above the IDA level, but not more than that of the Fund member with the highest income of those that were eligible to receive loans from the trust fund, receive subsidies at one-half the full rate. On the basis of data provided by the World Bank before April 30, 1982, eighty-eight developing member countries were eligible for the subsidies.[45] As of April 30, 1984, twenty-five countries had received SDR 217 million of subsidy payments.[46]

The primary source of financing for the subsidy account will be SDR 750 million of repayments and interest on trust fund loans. In addition, voluntary contributions in the form of donations and concessional loans, totaling SDR 52 million, had been made by eleven members (not including the United States) and Switzerland by April 30, 1984.[47]

44. IMF, *Annual Report, 1984*, p. 89. The beneficiaries were Bangladesh, Cameroon, the Central African Republic, Egypt, Haiti, India, the Ivory Coast, Kenya, Mali, Mauritania, Pakistan, Senegal, Sierra Leone, Sri Lanka, the Sudan, Tanzania, Western Samoa, the People's Democratic Republic of Yemen, Grenada, Malawi, Morocco, Papua New Guinea, the Philippines, Zaire, and Zambia.

45. IMF, *Annual Report, 1983*, pp. 103–04.

46. Countries receiving subsidies at the 3 percent rate were Bangladesh, Bolivia, Dominica, Gambia, Guyana, India, Kenya, Liberia, Madagascar, Malawi, Mauritania, Pakistan, the Philippines, Senegal, Sierra Leone, Sri Lanka, the Sudan, Tanzania, Togo, and Zambia. Recipients of subsidies at the 1.5 percent rate were the Ivory Coast, Jamaica, Mauritius, Morocco, and Peru. IMF, *Annual Report, 1984*, p. 91.

47. Ibid., p. 90.

### *Trust Fund Loans*

The trust fund, described earlier, was established in 1976. During the period that ended March 31, 1981, the trust fund made loans totaling SDR 2,991 million (not included in Fund credit, as defined earlier). No additional loans will be made.[48] The outstanding balance of trust fund loans on December 31, 1984, was SDR 2,770 million.[49]

### *Trust Fund Distribution of Profits from Gold Sales*

The distribution of profits from gold sales, previously described, amounted to SDR 1,003 million over the period 1978–80. The profits were distributed to developing countries in proportion to IMF quotas. The non-oil developing countries received 82.5 percent of the total, and the oil-exporting developing countries received the remaining 17.5 percent.[50]

### *Prolonged Use of IMF Credit*

The combination of special facilities and severe economic problems encountered by some countries in the 1960s and by many more countries in the 1970s and early 1980s resulted in prolonged use of IMF credit by a number of members. Table 2 shows that twenty-four member countries made use of Fund credit for periods of eleven continuous years or longer during the three decades ended in 1984. (The figures in the table are inexact for the reason given in footnote a; also, there may have been some short interruptions of use not revealed by the year-end figures.) In nineteen cases, the member was still using Fund credit at the end of 1984. Fourteen of the twenty-four countries making prolonged use of Fund credit belonged to the group of low-income countries that received trust fund loans.

The cases of prolonged continuous (or virtually continuous) use of IMF credit were attributable to unforeseen adverse external conditions or policy failures rather than to a deliberate decision of the Fund to extend the maturity of its credits. It is true that ten of the twenty-four countries listed in table 2 were granted credits under the extended Fund facility, which allows a period of repayment up to ten years, but the earliest of

48. IMF, *Annual Report, 1981*, p. 104.
49. IMF, *International Financial Statistics*, March 1985, p. 24.
50. IMF, *International Financial Statistics: Supplement on Fund Accounts,* no. 3 (1982), p. 11.

Table 2. *Members Making Prolonged Use of IMF Credit in the Period 1954–84*[a]

| *Member* | *Number of continuous years of use* | *Period* |
|---|---|---|
| Chile | 27 | 1958–84 |
| Egypt | 27 | 1958–84 |
| Sri Lanka | 22 | 1963–84 |
| Mali | 20 | 1965–84 |
| Sudan | 20 | 1965–84 |
| Pakistan | 19 | 1966–84 |
| Turkey | 18 | 1954–71 |
| Burma | 17 | 1968–84 |
| Nicaragua | 16 | 1969–84 |
| Philippines | 16 | 1969–84 |
| Guinea | 15 | 1970–84 |
| Chad | 14 | 1971–84 |
| Syria | 14 | 1961–74 |
| India | 13 | 1958–70 |
| Uganda | 13 | 1972–84 |
| Yugoslavia | 13[b] | 1972–84 |
| Zambia | 12 | 1972–84 |
| Afghanistan | 12 | 1965–76 |
| Bangladesh | 12 | 1973–84 |
| Indonesia | 12 | 1962–73 |
| Kampuchea, Democratic | 12 | 1973–84 |
| Zaire | 12 | 1973–84 |
| Jamaica | 11 | 1974–84 |
| Romania | 11 | 1974–84 |

Sources: International Monetary Fund, *International Financial Statistics: Supplement on Fund Accounts,* no. 3 (1982); IMF, *International Financial Statistics Yearbook, 1984;* IMF, *International Financial Statistics,* February 1985, pp. 22–23.

a. Periods of use are measured between the ends of calendar years and are, therefore, understated for all transactions occurring before December 31 of the years in question; the maximum understatement can approach two years.

b. Yugoslavia also had an eleven-year period of use from 1959 through 1969.

these was that of the Philippines in 1976. Hence, the cases of prolonged use reported in the table cannot be attributed mainly to the extended facility. They occurred as the result of a series of standby arrangements, often interspersed with drawings under the compensatory financing facility and sometimes followed in later years by an extended arrangement.[51] In general, the record is one of fluctuations in the amount of Fund credit

51. Democratic Kampuchea is an exception. Its only use of Fund credit was two drawings under the compensatory financing facility for export shortfalls, made in 1972 and 1973. The two drawings in the aggregate equaled 50 percent of the member's quota.

being used by the member country rather than a stable balance or a steadily growing one. In some cases, the outstanding amount of Fund credit fell to a low level during the period of continuous use. Some transactions, in effect, allowed rollovers of credits due for repayment. Before new standbys or other arrangements were agreed upon, the Fund had an opportunity to reassess the member's situation.

*Borrowing*

By borrowing the Fund has been able to offer certain special facilities and to permit larger drawings than could have been financed from its ordinary resources. Substantial amounts have been borrowed from member governments and their central banks and other official agencies and from the Swiss National Bank. The Fund has not borrowed in the market, though there is no legal barrier to doing so, and the possibility has been discussed.

A distinction should be made between borrowing through the GAB and other borrowing. Until the 1983 revisions, resources obtained through the GAB could be used only to finance drawings by the ten participating members. The arrangements were intended to ensure that the Fund could finance the drawings that could be made under the existing guidelines rather than to allow still larger credits. The drawings financed through the GAB have always been subject to the same charges as drawings from ordinary resources. Before the 1983 revisions, the interest rate paid to GAB lenders was based on the Fund's rate of charges, and the use of the GAB presumably was expected to be approximately self-financing, though this was not ensured.[52] In the future, the interest rate paid on Fund borrowings through the GAB will equal the combined market rate at which interest is paid on SDR holdings,[53] which now exceeds the rate of Fund charges.

Other borrowings have been used to finance the two oil facilities, the supplementary financing facility, the enlarged access policy, and (in part) the extended Fund facility. As mentioned earlier, the Fund's borrowing costs, plus a small margin, have been passed on to members using these facilities, though subsidies were provided for poor countries in the case of the 1975 oil facility and the supplementary financing facility. The imposi-

52. The interest rate paid to GAB lenders was subject to a 4 percent minimum, whereas drawings in the reserve tranche are free of charges. The most recent use of the GAB was for a reserve tranche purchase, equivalent to SDR 777 million, in November 1978 by the United States. See IMF, *Annual Report, 1983*, p. 94.

53. Ibid., p. 95.

tion of market-related charges for use of borrowed resources and a policy of raising regular charges toward market rates mark a movement away from an earlier concept (widely, but never universally, accepted) of the Fund as a cooperative organization in which members would temporarily extend or receive financing at low rates of remuneration and charges.

## The IMF and the World Bank

The relationship between the functions and lending policies of the IMF and its sister organization, the World Bank, has a significant bearing on the evaluation of proposals for channeling more economic assistance through the IMF to the developing countries. The Bretton Woods Conference, which settled on proposals for the establishment of the IMF, also proposed the creation of the World Bank to help finance postwar reconstruction and to serve the special credit needs of the less developed countries.

The Bank's development function was narrowly conceived in terms of lending for productive projects, from private sources with Bank guarantee or by the Bank with funds raised in the market. The Bank's Articles of Agreement provide that "Loans made or guaranteed by the Bank shall, except in special circumstances, be for the purpose of specific projects of reconstruction or development" [Article III, sec. 4 (vii)]. The U.S. Congress, nevertheless, in ratifying the agreement tried to make clear that the Bank, rather than the IMF, should make loans for "the reconstruction of monetary systems, including long-term stabilization loans." The Bank's executive directors agreed that in special circumstances such loans could be made by the Bank, and early loans to France, the Netherlands, Denmark, and Luxembourg came under this interpretation.[54]

The Bank later took the position that the early reconstruction loans were exceptional only in the sense that they were not preceded by a detailed examination of the specific projects for which the imports so financed were to be used. The executive directors held that the specific-project provision of the Articles was intended "simply to assure that Bank loans will be used for productive purposes" and that "In effect, the only requirement which it imposes is that, before a loan is granted, there shall be a clear agreement both on the types of goods and services for which

54. International Bank for Reconstruction and Development, *First Annual Report by the Executive Directors* (1946), pp. 12, 22–27; Edward S. Mason and Robert E. Asher, *The World Bank since Bretton Woods* (Brookings, 1973), pp. 11–25.

the proceeds of the loan are to be expended and on the uses to which those goods and services are to be put."[55]

World Bank financing has taken the form primarily of direct loans from resources obtained by borrowing in the market. Borrowers have been charged interest rates sufficient to cover the Bank's borrowing costs and operating expenses.

In 1960 the International Development Association (IDA) was established as an affiliate of the International Bank for Reconstruction and Development (IBRD) to provide credits for productive purposes to low-income countries on easy terms. IDA's resources come from contributions by member governments and transfers from the net earnings of the IBRD.

Despite the interpretation that the specific-project provision of the Articles imposes only a procedural requirement, the World Bank classifies its loans as project or nonproject on the basis of purpose. The Bank has stressed project lending but has made a considerable amount of nonproject loans. As of June 30, 1984, the cumulative amount of nonproject lending by the IBRD and IDA was $10.0 billion, equal to 7.4 percent of total lending.[56] According to the Bank's classification, project lending includes loans not only for specific productive installations but also for construction and capital equipment for narrow or broad economic sectors and credits for purposes such as education, health, technical assistance, and relending to small enterprises. Nonproject lending includes loans to finance imports of raw materials and intermediate products for economic sectors or the whole economy and some local-currency costs as well.[57]

In 1980 the Bank initiated structural adjustment lending, which was "designed to support major changes in policies and institutions of developing countries that would reduce their current-account deficits to more manageable proportions in the medium term while maintaining their maximum feasible development effort."[58] In 1983 this form of lending was incorporated in a broader special assistance program, which was established for two years. The program was "designed to help developing countries restore their development efforts despite adverse external cir-

55. International Bank for Reconstruction and Development, *Fifth Annual Report, 1949–1950*, p. 7.

56. World Bank, *The World Bank Annual Report, 1984*, pp. 208–09. In the fiscal year ended June 30, 1984, nonproject lending equaled 8.9 percent of the total. Ibid., pp. 144, 146.

57. Mason and Asher, *World Bank since Bretton Woods*, pp. 230–32; Stanley Please, *The Hobbled Giant: Essays on the World Bank* (Boulder, Colo.: Westview Press, 1984), pp. 9–12, 24; *World Bank Annual Reports*, various issues.

58. *World Bank Annual Report, 1981*, p. 69.

cumstances."[59] It had five major elements: (1) expanded structural adjustment lending; (2) sector adjustment support in the form of loans for export development, rehabilitation and modernization of existing facilities, and provision of agricultural inputs as part of a program to improve incentives; (3) financing of an increased share of project costs, including part of local-currency costs, especially in the poorest countries; (4) enhanced policy dialogue with members; and (5) coordination with other international lending institutions and bilateral aid donors. The Bank announced that it would be willing temporarily to allow structural adjustment loans to exceed the limit of 30 percent previously imposed on that component of its total lending to a country. It also intimated that it would be prepared to exceed the 10 percent limit previously imposed on structural adjustment loans in relation to its total lending.

As of June 30, 1984, the Bank had approved structural adjustment loans to sixteen countries totaling $4.5 billion.[60] Structural adjustment loans accounted for approximately one-third of all Bank lending to the recipient countries.

The introduction of structural adjustment lending by the World Bank and the establishment of the extended Fund facility by the IMF in 1974 involved each institution in a kind of lending that had previously been considered the primary responsibility of the other. The difference between the loans of the two organizations had never been precisely equivalent to a distinction between development finance and balance of payments finance. The great bulk of Bank lending is to pay for imports, and Fund credit enables member countries to avoid or lessen interruptions of their development programs. In the past, however, there was a significant pragmatic distinction related to the restrictions attached to the use of the credits.

The Bank's structural adjustment loans are generally free of restrictions on use of the proceeds that apply to its project loans and sector loans. The latter are extended to finance specified expenditures, and are disbursed as the expenditures are made. They typically require the receiving country to make additional expenditures to cover domestic currency costs. Although project loans and sector loans may strengthen the balance of payments in the future, they generally are not intended to help cover an immediate balance of payments deficit caused by adverse external conditions or policy errors. In marked contrast, structural adjustment

59. *World Bank Annual Report, 1983,* pp. 39–40.

60. The recipients were Kenya, Turkey, Bolivia, the Philippines, Senegal, Guyana, Mauritius, Malawi, the Ivory Coast, Korea, Thailand, Jamaica, Pakistan, Togo, Yugoslavia, and Panama.

loans generally supply foreign exchange that is freely usable except for certain prohibited purposes. In this respect, structural adjustment loans resemble Fund credits, which are freely disposable, subject only to the limitation that they may not be used "to meet a large or sustained outflow of capital" (Articles of Agreement, Article VI, sec. 1). Despite the fungibility of money, the degree to which credit use is restricted is important in many cases, especially for countries facing severe balance of payments difficulties.

In creating the extended facility the IMF moved toward the longer term lending of the World Bank. For drawings under the extended facility, the Fund agreed to lengthen the repayment schedule from the usual three to five years to a period of four to eight years (later extended to ten years). IBRD loans usually have a final maturity of fifteen to twenty years, with repayments of principal beginning about four to five years after disbursement. IDA credits are repayable over a period of ten to fifty years. Perhaps more indicative of the Fund's inclination to move toward the Bank's area was its statement that the extended facility was intended to assist members suffering from "slow growth and an inherently weak balance of payments position which prevents pursuit of an active development policy."[61]

The changes in the lending policies of the World Bank and the IMF appear to have brought with them some changes in the conditions attached to their credits. Part of the apparent changes, however, may reflect modifications of rhetoric rather than differences in substance. According to a senior vice president of the Bank, structural adjustment loans are supported by programs that include measures falling primarily within four areas: (1) the restructuring of incentives, including pricing policies, tariff reforms, taxation, budget subsidies, and interest rates; (2) the revision of public investment priorities; (3) improvements in budgeting and debt management; and (4) the strengthening of institutions, particularly public enterprises. The Bank reaches an understanding with the borrowing government on specific actions to be taken, and a few key actions are made preconditions for the release of disbursements. Satisfactory progress in carrying out the overall program is also a requirement.[62]

The Bank's concern with these subjects is not new. It had offered advice and technical assistance on them long before deciding to make structural adjustment loans. What is new is that acceptance of the Bank's

61. IMF, *Annual Report, 1975*, p. 88.

62. Ernest Stern, "World Bank Financing of Structural Adjustment," in John Williamson, ed., *IMF Conditionality* (Washington, D.C.: Institute for International Economics, 1983), pp. 93, 99. See also Please, *The Hobbled Giant*, pp. 28–34.

views on a broad range of institutional and policy matters has been made a condition for obtaining a structural adjustment loan.

The IMF, like the World Bank, has been accustomed to giving advice and technical assistance on a range of questions extending beyond its immediate operational requirements. The emphasis has been on macroeconomic policies related to aggregate bank credit, the fiscal deficit, external debt, and the exchange rate. Although a general review of policies precedes the approval of a standby arrangement or extended facility arrangement, performance criteria have usually been limited to a few macroeconomic variables and to the observance of what one writer has called "club rules" about exchange and payments practices.[63] The selection of performance criteria has been dictated by the principle of political neutrality and a desire to avoid too close an involvement in specific decisions relating to policy implementation. The observance of a global monetary aggregate has been the most common economic performance criterion.[64]

Supply-side language has appeared more often in Fund statements in recent years. Presumably, discussions of extended arrangements have devoted attention to structural changes to influence exports, imports, and import substitution. Programs probably have included nonbinding understandings on structural policies. The limited amount of information that is publicly available, however, suggests that there has been little, if any, change in the choice of performance criteria.[65]

Both the Fund and the World Bank have stressed the need for close collaboration, particularly in regard to energy policies, extended arrangements, and structural adjustment loans. A greater number of country missions have included staff members from both institutions. In documents on countries' adjustment programs that are submitted to each of the two boards, the position of the other institution is summarized. The Bank has taken the position that a stabilization program, normally supported by a Fund standby or extended arrangement, is needed as a foun-

63. "Panel Discussion: Richard N. Cooper," in Williamson, ed., *IMF Conditionality*, p. 574.

64. C. David Finch, "Adjustment Policies and Conditionality," in Williamson, ed., *IMF Conditionality*, p. 78.

65. Williamson usefully distinguishes between (a) preconditions, actions that must be taken before the board approves a standby or extended arrangement; (b) performance criteria; and (c) policy understandings concerning actions the country agrees to take but to which no explicit sanction for nonfulfillment is attached. See John Williamson, "The Lending Policies of the International Monetary Fund," in Williamson, ed., *IMF Conditionality*, p. 633. On four extended arrangements, see the following in Williamson, ed., *IMF Conditionality:* Kenya, 1975, pp. 397–98; Jamaica, 1978 and 1979, pp. 249, 253; and India, 1981, p. 520.

dation for a program for a structural adjustment loan. The Fund has relied on the Bank for the assessment of investment programs.[66]

No sharp line has been drawn between the roles of the Fund and the Bank on the basis of objectives, concern with the short run or the long run, or focus on macroeconomic or microeconomic questions. It is reasonable to expect, nevertheless, that the history of the two institutions and the expertise and experience of their staffs will continue to influence the scope of their policy advice and the conditions attached to their credits. Within overlapping ranges, the Fund may be expected to concentrate on demand management through the control of aggregate bank credit and the fiscal deficit, on the exchange and payments system, and on external debt problems, while the Bank emphasizes the level and composition of public investment, the organization and management of government agencies and public enterprises, and specific incentives for exports and import substitution. Close cooperation will be needed to avoid wasteful duplication of effort and inconsistent or conflicting advice.[67]

The complementary character of the Fund and the Bank has been recognized by the international community. From the outset, members of the Bank have been required to be members of the Fund. The common interest of the two institutions in the flow of resources to developing countries was recognized in 1974 by the establishment of a continuing Joint Ministerial Committee of the Boards of Governors of the World Bank and the International Monetary Fund on the Transfer of Real Resources to Developing Countries (Development Committee). Ministers and central bank governors of the Group of Ten countries in a communiqué issued after a meeting in May 1984 "stressed the need for closer cooperation between the IMF and the IBRD and noted the valuable contribution that the latter institution can make in fostering structural adjustment."[68]

## Possible Forms of Additional Economic Assistance through the IMF

This section examines the possibility of providing additional economic assistance to developing countries through existing facilities of the IMF

66. On the recent period, see Stern, "World Bank Financing of Structural Adjustment," p. 90. The earlier history of Fund-Bank relations is reviewed in de Vries, *The International Monetary Fund, 1966–1971*, vol. 1, pp. 610–15.

67. For a proposal for still closer collaboration between the Bank and the Fund, see Please, *The Hobbled Giant*, pp. 69–80.

68. *IMF Survey*, June 4, 1984, p. 168.

and in four possible additional forms—a subsidy for charges payable by low-income countries, a soft-loan facility, an SDR-aid link, and a facility for external debt relief. In the version here considered, the soft-loan facility would offer conditional credit. The SDR-aid link in its simplest form would supply unconditional liquidity, but some versions would associate the link with conditional credit. A debt-relief facility would be addressed to problems that are serious for some, but not all, developing countries and potentially threatening to the international financial system.

The liberalization of existing IMF facilities or the addition of new ones can be viewed as possible further steps in the evolution of the IMF. The approval of any of the proposals would have to await a substantial consensus, particularly among the large industrial countries. The currents of public and professional opinion, the political forces, and the negotiations that might produce agreement are not discussed here. That obstacles would have to be overcome is shown by the difficulties and delays with respect to the eighth quota review of the IMF and the seventh replenishment of IDA, both of which produced smaller increases than had been supported by many member countries.

### *Credits through Existing Facilities*

The amount of credit available from the IMF through existing facilities was increased after the increase in quotas provided by the eighth general review (effective November 30, 1983). The Fund's liquidity and its capacity to accommodate members' requests were improved by the quota increase (to a total of SDR 89.2 billion) and by the revised and enlarged General Arrangements to Borrow (to a total of SDR 17 billion, effective December 26, 1983). Supplementing the General Arrangements to Borrow was a line of credit from Saudi Arabia in the amount of SDR 1.5 billion. In addition, four short-term borrowing agreements for a total of SDR 6 billion were concluded with the Saudi Arabian Monetary Authority, the Bank for International Settlements, Japan, and the National Bank of Belgium (announced April 30, 1984).[69]

The 47 percent increase in quotas was much smaller than that advocated by prominent spokesmen for the developing countries. The Inter-

69. IMF, *Annual Report, 1984*, pp. 81–82. On April 30, 1984, SDR 2.3 billion remained uncommitted under a medium-term borrowing agreement for SDR 8.0 billion that had been concluded by the Fund with the Saudi Arabian Monetary Authority in 1981; further commitments could be made until May 1987.

Table 3. *IMF Quotas and International Trade, Non-Oil Developing Countries, Selected Years, 1954–84*

| *Year* | *Quotas, end of year (billions of SDRs)* | *Trade (billions of SDRs)* | *Ratio of quotas to trade*[a] *(percent)* |
|---|---|---|---|
| 1954 | 1.31 | 45.01 | 2.9 |
| 1959 | 2.43 | 55.69 | 4.4 |
| 1966 | 4.68 | 82.64 | 5.7 |
| 1970 | 6.68 | 110.93 | 6.0 |
| 1978 | 9.74 | 352.05 | 2.8 |
| 1980 | 16.59 | 559.89 | 3.0 |
| 1983 | 23.16 | 646.78 | 3.6 |
| 1984 | 23.46 | 707.16[b] | 3.3 |

Sources: IMF, *International Financial Statistics: Supplement on Fund Accounts,* no. 3 (1982), pp. 14–15; IMF, *International Financial Statistics Yearbook, 1983,* pp. 72–73, 76–77; IMF, *International Financial Statistics,* March 1985, p. 14.

a. The sum of exports and imports; dollar values converted to SDR values by application of the average SDR-to-dollar exchange rate for the period.

b. In four quarters ended September 30, 1984.

governmental Group of 24 on International Monetary Affairs and the Independent Commission on International Development Issues (the Brandt Commission) both proposed that quotas be at least doubled.[70]

For non-oil developing countries as a group, the enlarged quotas were greater in relation to their 1983 and 1984 international trade than IMF quotas had been during the late 1970s and early 1980s, but were smaller than they had been after some previous increases in quotas. Table 3 shows the ratios of quotas of the non-oil developing countries to their international trade for 1954 and 1984 and for the years in which the six general increases in quotas became effective.

The ratios are no more than a rough index of the availability of Fund credit in relation to needs because of changes in policies over time and changes in needs relative to international trade. Although Fund policies allow larger drawings in relation to quotas than at times in the past, the outstanding drawings of many countries are already at a high level. The structural problems, depressed state of trade, and other difficulties of the developing countries suggest that their need for Fund credit may be greater in relation to international trade than in the past. Since most developing countries maintain pegged exchange rates,[71] the abandonment of the Bretton Woods par value system has not materially reduced their need for balance of payments finance.

Under current policies, the availability of Fund credit will increase proportionately less than quotas. After the 1983 quota increase, the ex-

70. *IMF Survey*, February 21, 1983, pp. 52, 61.

71. IMF, *Annual Report, 1984*, p. 50.

ecutive board of the IMF revised the guidelines that relate access to Fund credit to a member's quota. Access limits for the enlarged access policy were lowered in percentage terms but, for most members, they increased somewhat in absolute amounts; for the compensatory financing facility, the cereal imports facility, and the buffer stock financing facility, the amount of access was increased relatively more.

The guidelines will be reviewed annually. The board stated that the guideline limits will not be regarded as targets, implying that credits equal to the limits should not be routinely approved. In exceptional circumstances, however, the Fund can approve standby or extended arrangements providing credit greater than the guideline limits.[72]

It may be advisable for the Fund to liberalize the guidelines or to interpret "exceptional circumstances" broadly. That would help some of the developing countries, but for others drawings as large as those allowed under present quantitative guidelines would be imprudent. Some of the poorest countries would face great difficulties in paying regular Fund charges or the higher charges for transactions financed by Fund borrowing and in achieving balance of payments surpluses sufficient to repay the Fund over the period of years prescribed by present policies. The Fund may have to restrict its credits to some of the most needy members unless a new facility is established for their benefit.

### *Subsidy for Charges Payable by Low-Income Countries*

A simple form of additional assistance to developing countries would be an explicit subsidy for charges for use of Fund credit. There are precedents for such assistance in the subsidies for the 1975 oil facility and the supplementary financing facility (described in preceding sections). A close parallel would be a subsidy for low-income countries covering part of the market-related cost of using borrowed resources under the enlarged access policy. A more liberal policy would be to apply the subsidy also to drawings financed by the Fund's ordinary resources.

72. For 1984 the access limits under the enlarged access policy (in relation to the new quotas, net of the excluded facilities) were set at 102–125 percent annually or 306–375 percent over a three-year period and a cumulative limit of 408–500 percent. For compensatory financing, the guideline limit was set at 83 percent of quota for export shortfalls and the same amount for cereal import excesses, subject to a limit of 105 percent if both forms of compensatory financing were used. For buffer stock financing, the maximum access was set at 45 percent of quota. See *IMF Survey*, January 9, 1984, pp. 7–8; IMF, *Annual Report, 1984*, pp. 130–35. For 1985, the access limits under the enlarged access policy were reduced to 95–115 percent annually, 280–345 percent over three years, and 408–450 percent cumulatively, and no change was made in the limits for the special facilities. *IMF Survey*, November 26, 1984, pp. 356–57.

The subsidy might be offered to member countries included in an updated version of the list of eighty-eight low-income countries that were eligible for the supplementary financing facility subsidy. An alternative and probably preferable standard would be to limit the subsidy to countries eligible for IDA assistance, thus adopting a criterion of need for subsidized credit that has gained wide international acceptance. According to World Bank statistics, sixty-four IMF member countries have low enough per capita income to qualify by the latter standard.[73]

The subsidy might be financed by voluntary contributions of member countries and from the uncommitted portion of the repayments of trust fund loans. Trust fund loans outstanding at the end of 1984 amounted to SDR 2.8 billion.[74] These loans are repayable in installments by 1991. SDR 750 million of receipts from repayments and interest on trust fund loans has been earmarked for the subsidy for the supplementary financing facility. The remaining SDR 2.0 billion would cover the periodic charges on an average amount of Fund credit of SDR 4.1 billion over the seven years 1985–91 (computed at the present 7 percent rate of charge), which is equal to 39 percent of the aggregate quotas of the sixty-four member countries eligible for IDA assistance. Although this would provide a significant amount of assistance, it would fall far short of covering total charges if average usage in relation to quotas should remain at the mid-1984 level (as of June 30, 1984, use of Fund credit by the sixty-four countries equaled 113 percent of their aggregate quotas; exclusive of India, the figure was 96 percent of aggregate quotas).

If additional economic assistance were provided through the IMF, a subsidy for charges would be an attractive possibility. There are precedents for this form of assistance and for limiting it to low-income countries. The assistance would be conditional on meeting the Fund's usual standards. It could be financed from uncommitted resources plus voluntary contributions. The subsidy could be put into effect quickly if agreement were reached about its desirability.

A subsidy scheme of the kind described, however, would have limitations. Although the subsidy would make it possible for some poor countries to draw larger amounts from the Fund than they otherwise could afford, it would not enlarge access limits or lengthen the repayment period. The repayments of trust fund loans would constitute only a temporary source of finance; after 1991, reliance would have to be placed on

73. Countries with per capita GNP of $806 or less in 1982 prices are eligible for IDA assistance. See *World Bank Annual Report, 1984*, p. 3. The Fund member countries in the class are listed in a footnote in the section on a soft-loan facility.

74. IMF, *International Financial Statistics*, February 1985, p. 24.

voluntary contributions or other sources. An intangible, but possibly important, factor is that the subsidy scheme would lack the symbolism attached to the establishment of a new facility, and would be less likely to stimulate fresh thinking about Fund policies and procedures.

### *A Soft-Loan Facility*

Consideration might be given to establishing on a more comprehensive, secure, and permanent basis a facility that could help meet the needs of poor countries, which have been recognized by the IMF in the past through certain special facilities and ad hoc subsidies and grants. Such a facility may be thought of as a soft-loan window analogous to the World Bank's IDA affiliate. It could be a new facility in the IMF or a separate account administered by the IMF; or, like IDA, it could be organized as a separate legal entity, but with the same executive directors, management, and staff as its parent institution.

Many variants are conceivable. The essential features of a soft-loan facility would be (1) its use would be limited to low-income developing countries; (2) access would be conditional on the pursuit of acceptable adjustment policies by the member country; (3) charges would be subsidized; and (4) the repayment period would be longer than for existing facilities except, perhaps, the extended facility. Credits extended through a soft-loan facility would supplement other Fund credits in a mix judged appropriate in light of a country's needs and economic capacity. For some, but not all, variants, it would be necessary to find a regular source of finance for the subsidies.

Although there is no reason to doubt the power of the Fund to set up still another special facility to deal with the problems of a particular group of countries, questions could arise concerning its power to adopt certain features of a soft-loan facility. These legal issues are not examined systematically in this paper, but some general remarks may be helpful. First, the Fund can administer special accounts or legal arrangements that are not subject to the same limitations as its ordinary operations. Precedents include the trust fund, the oil facility subsidy account, and the supplementary financing facility account.[75] Second, the Articles of Agree-

75. Article V, sec. 2(b) of the Fund Agreement states: "If requested, the Fund may decide to perform financial and technical services, including the administration of resources contributed by members, that are consistent with the purposes of the Fund. Operations involved in the performance of such financial services shall not be on the account of the Fund. Services under this subsection shall not impose any obligation on a member without its consent."

ment allow the use of profits from gold sales for operations that are not authorized by other provisions but that are consistent with the purposes of the Fund. They provide that "Under this subsection . . . balance of payments assistance may be made available on special terms to developing members in difficult circumstances, and for this purpose the Fund shall take into account the level of per capita income" [Article V, sec. 12 (f)(ii)]. The approval of an 85 percent majority of the voting power is required. Third, the Articles of Agreement have been amended twice and could be amended again, if necessary. Amendment, however, is time consuming and requires the agreement of three-fifths of the members having 85 percent of the total voting power [Article XXVIII (a)].

*Eligibility.* Probably the least contentious decision about eligibility for soft loans from the IMF would be to adopt the same per capita income criterion as applies to assistance from the World Bank's IDA affiliate. As mentioned in the preceding section, sixty-four IMF member countries would qualify by that standard.[76] These countries have only 12.1 percent of IMF quotas (of which 6.3 percentage points are the quotas of China, India, and Indonesia).

*Conditionality.* A soft-loan facility would be intended to ease the balance of payments problems of poor countries but not to enable them to avoid policy changes required for adjustment. Hence, use of the facility would be conditional on the IMF 's judgment that the member's policies and performance were appropriate.

The measures required would include provisions similar to those contained in standby and extended arrangements in the upper credit tranches. As mentioned in the previous section, the policies and measures usually include limiting bank credit expansion and reducing the fiscal deficit, correction of an overvalued exchange rate, limitation of short-term and medium-term external borrowing, and refraining from introducing or intensifying foreign exchange restrictions or import restrictions for balance of payments reasons. Other actions often included in Fund-

76. In ascending order of estimated GNP per capita in 1982: Democratic Kampuchea, Bhutan, Lao PDR, Chad, Bangladesh, Ethiopia, Nepal, Guinea-Bissau, Mali, Equatorial Guinea, Burma, Zaire, Afghanistan, Maldives, Malawi, Burkina Faso, Uganda, India, Rwanda, Burundi, Tanzania, Vietnam, Somalia, Haiti, Benin, the Central African Republic, the People's Republic of China, Guinea, Niger, Madagascar, Sri Lanka, Togo, Comoros, Vanuatu, Cape Verde, Ghana, Mozambique, Gambia, Sao Tome and Principe, Pakistan, Kenya, Sierra Leone, the Sudan, Mauritania, PDR Yemen, Djibouti, Liberia, Senegal, the Yemen Arab Republic, Lesotho, Bolivia, Indonesia, St. Vincent, the Solomon Islands, Western Samoa, Zambia, Honduras, Guyana, Egypt, El Salvador, Dominica, Grenada, St. Lucia, Thailand. Some of the estimates are for 1981. World Bank, *World Development Report, 1984*, pp. 218, 276; World Bank, *World Development Report, 1983*, pp. 148, 204.

supported adjustment programs (though not made performance criteria) are the establishment of positive real interest rates by removing ceilings on rates for government securities, savings accounts, and bank loans; the correction of price distortions by lifting controls and eliminating or modifying subsidies; and the strengthening of the fiscal system by tax revision and better budgeting. The adjustment programs are intended to improve the balance of payments by reducing excess demand, by encouraging production of export goods and import substitutes, and by attracting foreign investment and aid.

Critics have raised a variety of objections to IMF-sponsored adjustment programs as they affect developing countries.[77] Some of the objections relate to technical questions about the efficacy of measures recommended by the Fund and their influence on development. Although these questions merit further study and discussion, a consideration of them is outside the scope of this paper. Other criticisms assert that IMF programs are too harsh in terms of the magnitude and speed of adjustment. It is alleged that the programs involve reductions in the standard of living that are unacceptable for humanitarian reasons or that pose threats to political stability and that they unduly retard economic growth. A related criticism is that Fund programs fail to distinguish fairly between balance of payments difficulties caused by external factors and those caused by poor policies.

The essential content of balance of payments adjustment is the pursuit of policies that will eliminate an unsustainable external deficit. For a developing country, this means that the deficit on merchandise trade and services should not exceed the dependable inflow of private and official capital and aid. Fund credit allows countries to spread the adjustment effort over a longer period than otherwise would be possible, but to meet charges and to repay the Fund, the member country has to achieve a surplus in the other parts of its balance of payments.

A soft-loan facility could help members in two ways. First, by offering larger amounts of Fund credit and a longer adjustment period, the severity of necessary measures could be lessened, provided that other credit and aid did not decline because of the change in Fund policies. In programs supporting soft loans, as in programs for extended arrangements, more reliance could be placed on adjustment through increased output in

77. See, for example, Williamson, ed., *IMF Conditionality*; Tony Killick, ed., *Adjustment and Financing in the Developing World: The Role of the International Monetary Fund* (Washington, D.C.: IMF, and London: Overseas Development Institute, 1982); Bahram Nowzad, *The IMF and Its Critics*, Essays in International Finance 146 (Princeton University, 1981).

the form of import substitutes and exports than is usually possible in the Fund's traditional short-term programs, which frequently require a reduction of aggregate demand. Second, by providing for lower charges and a relatively long repayment period, a soft-loan facility could lessen the size and defer the date of the required surplus in the other external transactions. The grant element in the transaction could be increased.

For a soft-loan facility, as for the extended facility, a general program covering a period of years could be formulated, and detailed programs for each year could be worked out later. Drawings could be phased over the whole period. A maximum period of five years might be appropriate. During the disbursement period, failure to observe the conditions included in the program would interrupt access to further drawings.

A successful soft-loan facility would enable the IMF to extend more credit to some of the poorest countries than would now be appropriate even in exceptional circumstances in which the normal guidelines for the size of drawings in relation to quota would be waived. The larger grant element attributable to easier terms for charges and repayment would lessen the danger that these countries could meet their obligations to the Fund only by constraining their consumption and investment to levels that would be unacceptable to them and to the international community.

The establishment of a soft-loan facility would not directly address the issue of differences in the origin of balance of payments difficulties. The IMF already tries to take account of the differences in deciding which policy changes the country has to make. When the problem is judged to be primarily external in origin and temporary in nature, only minimal policy changes may be required; if, however, it is attributable either to a lasting deterioration in external markets or natural conditions or to poor policies, policy changes to reduce the balance of payments deficit are required. The introduction of a soft-loan facility would justify a more relaxed attitude only to the extent that it made acceptable a somewhat more elastic definition of temporariness owing to a longer program period and slower repayments.

*Charges and repayment period.* By various combinations of rates of charge and repayment periods, a considerable range in the grant element of the soft-loan facility could be obtained. A precedent can be found in the terms of the trust fund loans, which were extended in 1977–81. These carry an interest rate of 0.5 percent per annum and are repayable in semiannual installments from six to ten years after the time of disbursement. At a 12 percent discount rate, these terms imply a 56.5 percent grant element. Extension of the repayment period to fifteen years would increase the grant element to 65.3 percent. These figures contrast with a grant element of 15.6 percent in ordinary drawings in the credit tranches, given the present 7.0 percent rate of charge, and a smaller grant component in the future if the Fund's announced policy of raising the remuneration rate relative to market interest rates is accompanied by an increase in charges. For transactions financed from borrowed resources, which have accounted for almost half of Fund credit through extended arrangements, the grant element is smaller than it is for ordinary drawings.

If a soft-loan facility were made an integral part of the IMF, the question could be raised whether a repayment period longer than ten years would be consistent with the provision of the Articles of Agreement requiring the establishment of "adequate safeguards for the temporary use of the general resources of the Fund" [Article V, sec. 3(a)]. This provision would not necessarily apply if the facility took the form of a separate legal entity or a separate legal arrangement, which would not operate with the Fund's general resources.

*Financing.* The additional credits extended under a soft-loan facility might come from the Fund's ordinary resources or from borrowing, the sale of gold, relending part of the receipts from repayments of trust fund loans, or an SDR allocation that high-income and middle-income member countries would agree to devote to that purpose.

The Fund's liquid ordinary resources amounted to approximately SDR 43 billion at the end of 1984, consisting of about SDR 38 billion of usable currencies and SDR 5 billion of SDR holdings in the general department.[78] At the end of 1984 the Fund 's unused borrowing capacity under lines of credit supporting the enlarged access policy barely exceeded the undrawn balances under existing standby arrangements and extended arrangements. SDR 18.5 billion was available under the General Arrangements to Borrow and the associated arrangement with Saudi Arabia, but this could be used only to finance credits to GAB participants or for credits to other countries in exceptional conditions threatening the stability of the international monetary system.

In addition to its liquid resources, on December 31, 1984, the IMF held gold amounting to SDR 32.5 billion, valued at market prices. Repay-

78. The figure for SDR holdings of the general department is from IMF, *International Financial Statistics*, February 1985, p. 38. The figure for holdings of usable currencies is a rough estimate derived by adjusting the figure for April 30, 1984 (published in IMF, *Annual Report, 1984*, p. 80), for changes in outstanding use of Fund credit, Fund borrowing, and the general department's holdings of SDRs. It is assumed that no changes were made between April 30, 1984, and December 31, 1984, in the list of countries whose currencies were considered usable.

ments of trust fund loans will provide uncommitted resources of approximately SDR 2.0 billion by 1991 (after allowance for the SDR 750 million earmarked for the subsidy for the supplementary financing facility).[79]

Careful study, including detailed projections and simulations, would be necessary to arrive at estimates of the resources that would be needed for various versions of a soft-loan facility. Such estimates will not be attempted here, but some facts about countries that might be eligible can be mentioned. The sixty-one low-income countries other than India, China, and Indonesia that would be eligible according to the IDA standard have IMF quotas totaling SDR 5.2 billion. Loans equal to 100 percent of the aggregate quotas of the sixty-one countries would come to about 12 percent of the liquid ordinary resources of the IMF under existing arrangements, or about 7 percent of these resources plus the market value of the Fund's gold and the uncommitted balance of outstanding trust fund loans. As of December 31, 1984, use of Fund credit (exclusive of drawings under the compensatory financing and buffer stock facilities) by the sixty-one low-income countries equaled 116 percent of their aggregate quotas. Hence, to raise their average use of Fund credit to 400 percent of quota (close to the maximum provided by current guidelines for the enlarged access policy) would entail drawings of SDR 14.8 billion. For the thirty poorest member countries (those with per capita GNP of $340 or less in 1982 prices), all the figures would be somewhat less than half of those for the group of sixty-one.

To the extent that soft loans were made from the Fund's general resources, it would be necessary either to provide separate financing for the subsidy for charges or to amend the Articles of Agreement to modify a requirement that charges be uniform for all members [Article V, sec. 8(d)]. The uniformity provision would not necessarily apply to loans from special resources contributed by member countries or profits from gold sales or to loans extended through a separate legal entity administered by the Fund. A subsidy might be financed by voluntary contributions, gold sales, or income from operations. The Fund's net income, after payment of remuneration to members whose currencies were being used and interest on borrowings, totaled SDR 310 million in the four financial years ended April 30, 1981, 1982, 1983, and 1984.[80]

A case could be made for raising charges for ordinary transactions in relation to market interest rates and in relation to the rate of remuneration as the latter is brought up toward the market-related SDR interest

79. IMF, *International Financial Statistics*, February 1985, pp. 24, 46.
80. IMF, *Annual Report, 1983*, p. 187; *Annual Report, 1984*, p. 164.

rate. Such a change would yield additional income that might be devoted in part to financing the subsidy for soft-loan charges. That arrangement would imply that relatively high-income developing countries, which would not be eligible for the soft-loan facility, would bear a large share of the cost of the subsidy, since they can be expected to continue to be heavy users of Fund credit.

Although the use of net income to subsidize a soft-loan facility would not appear to violate any express provision of the Articles of Agreement, it might be argued that an affirmative amendment would be needed to permit such use. Net income may be distributed or added to a general reserve or special reserve [Article XII, sec. 6(a)]; the Articles do not limit the use that the Fund may make of the general reserve, and the only use of the special reserve that they prohibit is its distribution to members. On April 30, 1984, the general and special reserves amounted to SDR 1,074 million, equal to 38 percent of the operational income for the fiscal year ended on that date.[81]

*Possible advantages and problems.* A distinctive feature of an IMF soft-loan facility of the kind outlined earlier is that its use would be subject to Fund conditionality. To obtain assistance, a country would have to present an adjustment program acceptable to the Fund and undertake to follow improved economic policies. Its performance would be monitored regularly, and disbursements of successive installments of credit would be contingent upon meeting specified criteria or further consultations with the Fund. These procedures would minimize the risk of misuse. To the extent that the adjustment program succeeded, both the borrower and other countries would benefit. These characteristics account for the principal advantage of an IMF soft-loan facility as a channel for additional economic assistance to low-income countries.

An objection that might be raised against the establishment of an IMF soft-loan facility is that it would duplicate the World Bank's lending. As noted in the preceding section, a problem of coordination already exists. The subject will be discussed further in the concluding section.

Another possible objection is that a soft-loan program attached to the IMF is unnecessary because donor countries can supplement Fund financing with bilateral aid and have done so for several countries. Although in some cases the combination of bilateral aid and Fund financing may have results similar to those that could be obtained by an IMF soft-loan facility, there is no assurance that appropriate amounts of con-

81. IMF, *Annual Report, 1984*, pp. 164–65.

cessional assistance will be made available on a nondiscriminatory and well-coordinated basis.

The establishment of a facility with eligibility related explicitly to per capita income could be divisive. Although the IMF has introduced several facilities (mainly or exclusively) to serve the needs of developing countries, generally this did not involve formal departure from uniform treatment of members. However, trust fund loans and the subsidy for the supplementary financing facility did entail distinctions based on per capita income, and they seem to have been well accepted. The subsidy for the oil facility was limited to poor countries, though they were not identified exclusively on the basis of per capita income. In the distribution of gold profits, a distinction was drawn between a broad class of developing countries and other members, but as earlier noted some countries with comparatively high per capita incomes were included (though a few of them returned part or all of their share of the profits).

It could be argued that factors other than per capita income should be taken into account in determining eligibility for a soft-loan facility. The degree of access to international capital markets and receipts of aid from sources other than the IMF might be considered especially relevant. The application of the former criterion, however, might be thought to involve too large an element of judgment and the latter criterion to have the effect of partly counteracting or offsetting decisions reached in other multilateral or bilateral aid programs.

Special problems would be posed by India, the People's Republic of China, and Indonesia. These countries presumably would meet the eligibility standards but, by virtue of size, they might absorb a large proportion of the resources of a soft-loan facility. This issue has arisen in connection with IDA. In addition, Indonesia is a major oil exporter.

The establishment of a soft-loan facility might be viewed as a relaxation of financial discipline and undue weakening of IMF conditionality. In practice, it might be difficult for the Fund staff and management actually to apply the usual standards of conditionality to a soft-loan facility since that inevitably would deprive some needy member countries of benefits. To be sure, the World Bank appears to succeed in applying common standards for IDA loans and other loans, but the number and variety of potential Bank loans to a member country, many of them for relatively small projects, tend to defuse the confrontation implied by refusal of an application. In contrast, a Fund refusal of a request for a drawing implies an unfavorable judgment about the country's policies as a whole and may impair its access to other credit and aid. If the Bank's structural adjustment loans should become a greater part of its total lending to particular countries, and if the conditional terms should begin to receive more publicity, the difference between the interpretation of lending decisions of the Bank and the Fund undoubtedly would diminish.

*Special Drawing Rights with a Link to Aid or Development Finance*

An extended debate on the desirability of creating a new international reserve asset culminated in 1969 with the adoption of an amendment to the IMF's Articles of Agreement authorizing special drawing rights. A recurrent issue in the discussions was whether reserve creation should be linked with aid or development finance. An early nonofficial proposal, advanced in 1960 and modified in 1962, would have allocated the additional reserves only to developing countries through IDA, and would have allowed industrial countries to earn the new reserves by exports to the developing countries.[82] Various other proposals were made for preferential allocations to less developed countries, either directly or indirectly. A contrary position was that new reserve assets should go only to the major industrial countries, which had special responsibilities and needs.[83] The outcome was that allocations were made to all participating members in proportion to Fund quotas.

The question of the desirability of a link, however, was not finally settled. Debate about it continued in connection with the discussion of international monetary reform during the 1970s[84] and may be reopened if large new allocations of SDRs should be seriously considered.

It is uncertain whether and when additional allocations of SDRs will be made. The considerations determining those decisions are not discussed here. It is assumed that substantial new allocations may be agreed upon at some time in the future, and the desirability of a link with aid or development finance in that event is examined.

82. Maxwell Stamp, "The Stamp Plan—1962 Version," in Herbert G. Grubel, ed., *World Monetary Reform: Plans and Issues* (Stanford University Press, 1963), pp. 80–89.

83. de Vries, *The International Monetary Fund, 1966–1971*, vol. 1, pp. 19, 56–57, 78–84, 110–11, 197, passim.

84. "Report of Technical Group on the SDR/Aid Link and Related Proposals," in International Monetary Fund, *International Monetary Reform: Documents of the Committee of Twenty* (IMF, 1974), pp. 95–111; Y. S. Park, *The Link between Special Drawing Rights and Development Finance*, Essays in International Finance (Princeton University, 1973); William R. Cline, *International Monetary Reform and the Developing Countries* (Brookings, 1976), pp. 50–57; George M. von Furstenberg, ed., *International Money and Credit: The Policy Issues* (IMF, 1983), pp. 498–502.

*Description of the SDR.* The Articles of Agreement of the IMF provide that in allocating or canceling SDRs "the Fund shall seek to meet the long-term global need, as and when it arises, to supplement existing reserve assets in such manner as will promote the attainment of its purposes and will avoid economic stagnation and deflation as well as excess demand and inflation in the world." Allocations, which can be authorized only by an 85 percent majority, must equal uniform percentages of the Fund quotas of participating members. Participants receive interest on their net holdings of SDRs and pay interest on their cumulative net allocations at equal and uniform rates.[85] For a member whose holdings equal its cumulative net allocations—in other words, a member that is neither a net user nor a net recipient of SDRs—the interest receipts and payments cancel out. Net users must make net payments and countries whose holdings exceed their allocations receive net payments. Although participation in the SDR department is optional, all Fund members have elected to take part. SDRs may be held not only by participating member countries but also by other countries, the Fund's general department, and official institutions prescribed by the Fund.

Until mid-1974 the interest rate on the SDR was fixed at 1.5 percent. Thereafter, it was pegged to the combined rate on certain liquid short-term obligations of high quality in member countries and was increased in relation to that rate in four steps. Since May 1981 the interest rate has been 100 percent of the combined weighted average rate in the five countries whose currencies make up the valuation basket for the SDR (the United States, the Federal Republic of Germany, France, Japan, and the United Kingdom). In 1983 the average interest rate was 8.49 percent; in 1984 it was 8.92 percent.

The use of SDRs is no longer subject to certain restrictions that were originally applied. The "reconstitution" provision (which required participants to maintain average holdings equal to at least a certain percentage of net cumulative allocations) has been suspended, and the requirement of a balance of payments need for use applies only in instances when the Fund designates the recipient. Participating countries are required to accept SDRs through designated transactions until their holdings reach three times their allocations. Transactions in SDRs also may be conducted by agreement between countries without limit. SDRs must be used to pay Fund charges and may be used to pay Fund quota subscriptions and to repay Fund credit.

Allocations of SDRs have been smaller and less regular than had been

85. These provisions appear in Articles XVIII and XX.

Table 4. *Holdings of Special Drawing Rights, December 31, 1984*

| *Holders* | *Amount (millions)* | *Percent of holders' cumulative allocations* |
|---|---|---|
| Industrial countries | 13,361[a] | 92.5 |
| Oil-exporting developing countries | 1,713 | 114.7 |
| Non-oil developing countries | 1,395 | 25.4 |
| IMF general department | 4,957 | . . . |
| Other holders | 14 | . . . |

Source: *International Financial Statistics,* February 1985, pp. 36, 39, 24.
a. Includes Switzerland.

expected. SDR 9.3 billion was allocated in the three years 1970–72 and an additional SDR 12.1 billion in the three years 1979–81.

At the end of 1984 the total of SDR 21.4 billion that had been issued was distributed among holders as shown in table 4. Most countries held less than their cumulative allocations. Among industrial countries and oil exporters, only Saudi Arabia, Kuwait, Libya, and Japan held more than twice as much as their cumulative allocations. A few small developing countries (Singapore, Malta, Paraguay, Trinidad and Tobago, Bahrain, and the Solomon Islands) also held more than twice their cumulative allocations. Many developing countries held small amounts or none. The Fund's general department held almost a quarter of cumulative total allocations.

*Economic gains of recipients.* Link proposals may be regarded as a way of favoring less developed countries in the distribution of the primary benefits from the creation of SDRs. Like issuing fiat money of a national state, the creation of SDRs involves a social saving compared with using gold or other commodity money. This saving may be called seigniorage. If no interest were paid or charged on SDRs, the seigniorage would accrue entirely to the recipients of the original allocation. When interest is paid and charged, the seigniorage accrues partly in proportion to original allocations and partly in proportion to subsequent holdings. The higher the interest rate, the smaller the former share and the larger the latter share. The increase of the SDR interest rate to the full combined interest rate has greatly reduced, but not eliminated, the gains original recipients can obtain by using their allocations.

SDR allocations provide a net positive financial inflow only so long as new allocations exceed a country's interest payments on its cumulative use of SDRs. But the gain associated with using SDRs obtained by direct

Table 5. *Illustration of Gain from Using SDRs Obtained by Direct Allocation, with Alternative Reference Interest Rates, 1984*[a]

| *Reference interest rate (percent per year)* | *Gain (percent of amount used)* |
|---|---|
| London Interbank Offer Rate (LIBOR), 10.85 percent[b] | 17.8 |
| LIBOR plus 1.5 percent, 12.35 percent[b] | 27.8 |
| Conventional rate of 10 percent used to calculate grant element in official loans | 10.8 |
| 15 percent | 40.5 |
| 20 percent | 55.4 |

Source: Author's calculations.
a. No allowance for commitment charge or grace period; SDR interest rate, 8.92 percent (average, 1984).
b. LIBOR for three-month U.S. dollar deposits (average, 1984), from IMF, *International Financial Statistics,* March 1985, p. 62.

allocation is not annulled at that point. The gain associated with net use of SDRs, $G$ (valued in SDRs), can be measured as

$$G = [(r - i)/r]\, Q,$$

where $r$ is a reference interest or discount rate for the country, $i$ is the SDR interest rate, and $Q$ is the amount used.[86] The gain or subsidy is equal to the present value, in perpetuity, of the difference between the interest payable on SDR use and the return on the resources obtained (or the interest saved on foreign debt), discounted at the reference interest rate. The formula makes no allowance for the possibility that the SDR use will be reversed in the future.

Selection of a reference interest rate is a matter of judgment. The reference rate may be equated with the rate that the country pays or would pay on long-term external loans or with the marginal rate of return on real assets in the country. The gain or subsidy element in using SDRs obtained by a direct allocation is illustrated in table 5, with an SDR interest rate of 8.92 percent (the average for 1984), in connection with various reference interest rates. The gain is greatest for those countries whose reference interest rate exceeds the SDR rate by the widest margin either because they must pay high interest rates to obtain foreign loans or because their rate of return on real investments is high.

The SDR interest rate has recently exceeded the interest rate on many official loans. In 1983, when the SDR interest rate averaged 8.5 percent,

86. For a clear and detailed exposition, see Herbert G. Grubel, "Basic Methods for Distributing Special Drawing Rights and the Problem of International Aid," *Journal of Finance*, vol. 27 (December 1972), pp. 1009–22.

the average interest rate on new medium-term and long-term loan commitments of official creditors to developing countries was 7.7 percent. Calculated with a conventional reference interest rate of 10 percent, the grant element was 17.6 percent of the loans, which totaled $34.6 billion. For low-income African countries and low-income Asian countries, the grant element in new official loan commitments was 57.8 percent and 57.2 percent, respectively.[87] The comparable figure for SDR use in 1983 was 15.1 percent (calculated with the conventional 10 percent reference interest rate). If calculated with a more realistic, higher reference interest rate, the grant elements in both official loans and SDR use would have been larger, but the gain from a representative official loan would still have been greater.

Countries that do not use their SDR allocations or that reverse their use nevertheless obtain a gain in the form of what may be called a liquidity yield. Receipt of SDR allocations relieves countries with depleted reserves of the need to restore their reserves and makes them more creditworthy.[88] Countries that voluntarily hold SDRs in excess of their cumulative allocations presumably do so because they consider the SDR an attractive reserve asset.

*Possible forms of link.* Several forms of link between SDRs and aid or development finance can be visualized: (1) allocations to developing countries exclusively or in amounts exceeding their proportionate share of Fund quotas; (2) allocations to development finance institutions for lending to developing countries at below-market interest rates; (3) allocation to the general department of the IMF for use in lending to developing countries; (4) a low, preferential SDR interest rate payable by developing countries on their net use of SDRs. For the fourth form of link, the difference between the interest paid by the selected users and the interest received by the holders of the SDRs might be covered by issuing additional SDRs.

In direct form, any of the versions of a link would require amendment of the IMF Articles of Agreement. But it might be possible to obtain some of the effects of the link methods through voluntary agreement among developed countries to pass on part or all of future SDR alloca-

87. World Bank, *World Debt Tables: External Debt of Developing Countries, 1984–85*, pp. 2–3, 7, 11.

88. John Williamson argues that a general SDR allocation in proportion to Fund quotas would be especially advantageous to capital-importing developing countries because they suffer from a reserve shortage. See John Williamson, *A New SDR Allocation?* Policy Analyses in International Economics 7 (Washington, D.C.: Institute for International Economics, March 1984), pp. 25–26.

tions to development finance institutions, or to the Fund for the special benefit of the less developed countries, or to subsidize the interest rate paid by the latter. The first of these voluntary methods has been called an "inorganic" or "indirect" link as distinguished from a straightforward "organic" link.

An issue that would be certain to arise in connection with any link proposal would concern the standards for eligibility (see comments on a soft-loan facility).

*Arguments in favor of a link.* The basic argument in favor of a link is that the distribution of the social saving or seigniorage resulting from a collective decision to create SDRs should favor the poor countries rather than the rich ones. A link would add to the small number of methods available for reducing inequalities of per capita income among countries. The present allocation method (on the basis of IMF quotas) provides much larger per capita amounts for rich countries than for poor ones. For example, although the IMF quotas of India and the Netherlands (SDR 2,207.7 million and SDR 2,264.8 million, respectively) are nearly equal, India's quota is only SDR 3.1 per capita while the Netherlands's quota is SDR 158.3 per capita (mid-1982 population figures).[89] This point, however, must be qualified by the observation that usually the poor countries enjoy a larger gain for each SDR used because the interest rates they pay on external borrowing are higher than those paid by the rich countries.

Some poor countries have difficulty in borrowing abroad because lenders are not acquainted with them or perceive them to be poor credit risks. These countries would benefit especially from a link. If the link took the form of channeling SDRs through development finance institutions or the Fund, the risk of misuse of resources, which may justify a poor credit rating in some cases, would be reduced and shared.

A link could provide aid or development finance without imposing an overt budgetary cost or balance of payments burden on rich countries. If, however, the link took the form of voluntary contributions of SDRs, the donors would remain liable for interest charges on their net cumulative allocations. To a considerable extent, the absence of budgetary cost and

89. Per capita IMF quotas are only loosely related to per capita income. Among twenty industrial countries, the correlation between per capita quotas and per capita GNP is low ($r = 0.15$). Among 103 non-oil developing countries, there is a positive but not very close relationship ($r = 0.62$). These statements relate to IMF quotas as of December 31, 1983, converted to per capita amounts on the basis of mid-1981 population, and to per capita GNP in 1981 (in SDRs). IMF quotas and SDR/dollar exchange rates are from IMF, *International Financial Statistics*, February 1984, pp. 14–17; income and population data are from World Bank, *World Development Report, 1983*, pp. 148–49, 204.

balance of payments burden for other forms of link would be a matter of appearance or presentation; any real resources gained by developing countries would come from other countries. Nevertheless, the characteristics of a link might be advantageous at times. In the United States, for example, the existence of a substantial amount of off-budget lending for domestic purposes suggests that such arrangements are politically attractive. From a strict economic standpoint, moreover, the gains of the poor countries could exceed the opportunity costs of the rich countries because the margin between the SDR interest rate and the reference interest rate is wider in the poor countries (if judged by the interest rate paid on external loans but less clearly so if judged by the marginal rate of return on real domestic investment).

Another argument advanced in favor of the link during the discussions of international monetary reform in the 1970s was that it would improve the quality of aid because the transfer of resources would not be tied to expenditure in any particular country, as bilateral aid often is.[90]

*Arguments against a link.* The main argument against a link is that decisions on allocations of SDRs and the characteristics of the SDR and on assistance to developing countries should be made separately on the basis of the considerations especially pertinent to them. Whereas SDR allocations should respond to global needs for additional reserves, official development assistance should be based on the absorptive capacity of recipients and the willingness of developed countries to provide aid. The characteristics of the SDR, particularly the interest rate, should be set to make SDR holdings competitive with other reserve assets and to make the SDR department of the Fund self-supporting, rather than to assist net users.

A second argument against a link is that it would politicize decisions on SDR allocations. Usually, the objection is that the existence of a link would make it difficult to withhold allocations—or to cancel part of past

90. For statements of arguments in favor of a link, see "Report of Technical Group on the SDR/Aid Link and Related Proposals"; John Williamson, "Surveys in Applied Economics: International Liquidity," *Economic Journal*, vol. 83 (September 1973), pp. 727–31; John Williamson, "SDRs: The Link," in Jagdish N. Bhagwati, ed., *The New International Economic Order: The North-South Debate* (MIT Press, 1977), pp. 81–100; and Alexandre Kafka, "Comment," in ibid., pp. 101–04; and other sources mentioned in Robert E. Cumby, "Special Drawing Rights and Plans for Reform of the International Monetary System: A Survey," in von Furstenberg, ed., *International Money and Credit*, pp. 457–60, 461–73. On the difference between the gains of beneficiaries and the costs borne by other countries, see the general discussion in Leipziger, "Lending Versus Giving" and "The Concessionality of Foreign Assistance."

allocations—when total liquidity was excessive because to do so would be interpreted as evidence of lack of sympathy with the developing countries. This argument appears weak so long as an 85 percent majority is required to approve an allocation. An opposite interpretation, less frequently advanced but less easily countered, is that developed countries will support allocations when needed for reserve purposes only if they continue to share in the benefits as fully as they have until now.

A third argument, advanced in the early discussions, is that a link would impair confidence in the SDR because it would cause a default risk. This objection has lost force owing to the suspension of the reconstitution requirement and the recognition that the quality of the SDR as an asset depends on its wide acceptability and the attractiveness of the interest rate rather than on any "backing" for it. There is still, however, a residual risk that at some point net users of SDRs may fail to pay interest.

A fourth argument is that allocations favoring the developing countries would involve a greater risk of inflation than allocations in proportion to Fund quotas because developing countries would use their allocations more quickly and more fully than would developed countries. The assumption about use no doubt is correct, but the inflationary impact probably would be minimal or nonexistent because of the small size of allocations in comparison with relevant magnitudes such as world GNP, international trade, and the monetary base; compensating reductions in borrowing from banks; and the capacity of national authorities to take offsetting action if required to contain inflation.

A fifth objection to a link is that it would fail to increase aid because developed countries would reduce other forms of official assistance enough to offset its effect. This argument points in the opposite direction from the second and third objections summarized earlier. The extent of offsetting reductions in other forms of aid likely would depend partly on the form of the link; offsetting probably would be greatest for versions entailing voluntary contributions to development institutions or voluntary payments to subsidize SDR interest rates.

A sixth criticism of a link in the form of direct allocations to developing countries in proportion to IMF quotas or a preferential interest rate on SDR use is that there would be no assurance that the assistance would go to the low-income countries with the most pressing needs or that it would be used effectively to promote balance of payments adjustment and growth. This form of aid would differ fundamentally from the conditional assistance that would be provided by an IMF soft-loan facility as described in the preceding section or by versions of the link that would channel the resources through development finance institutions or the general department of the IMF.[91]

*An External Debt-Relief Facility*

In 1982–83 the external debt problems of developing countries became increasingly severe owing to the worldwide recession, high real rates of interest, and curtailment of new lending by private financial institutions and, in many cases, to the cumulative effects of poor policies. The vulnerability of borrowers to adverse external developments was aggravated by increasing dependence during the 1970s on commercial bank loans with variable interest rates, rather than direct investment or official financing, and on loans with short maturities. Two groups of countries suffered especially—some of the major borrowers and low-income African countries.

The problems eased somewhat in 1984 as the gross domestic product and exports of developing countries increased and debt rescheduling agreements became effective. But not all countries participated in the recovery. Real interest rates on dollar debts, the major part of the total, increased in 1984. External debt transactions, which had resulted in net transfers to developing countries (excess of receipts from loan disbursements over payments for debt service) averaging $30 billion a year in 1978–81, appear to have turned negative in 1984 after declining sharply in 1982–83.[92]

The external liabilities of developing countries continued to increase in 1984 but at a slower rate than in preceding years (and apparently at a slower rate than exports). The estimated total reached $895 billion at the end of 1984 (including public and private short-term and long-term debt and use of IMF credit). Well over half of the long-term debt included in this total was owed by twelve major borrowers (Argentina, Brazil, Chile, Egypt, India, Indonesia, Israel, Korea, Mexico, Turkey, Venezuela, and Yugoslavia).[93]

91. For references to arguments against the link, see note 90. See also Cline, *International Monetary Reform and the Developing Countries*, pp. 58–91.

92. World Bank, *World Debt Tables: External Debt of Developing Countries, 1984–85*, pp. xi, xiii–xiv. The figures for net transfers relate to the 104 countries reporting to the World Bank under its debtor reporting system (DRS); the figure for 1984 is a preliminary estimate.

93. Ibid., pp. ix, xi. These figures include not only the statistics for the 104 DRS countries but also estimates for other developing countries; high-income oil exporters are not included.

Many countries have had to reschedule their external debts in recent years. Initially, rescheduling was regarded as a stopgap response to acute liquidity problems and usually dealt with debt service of only a one-year period. Lately, it seems to have come to be accepted as a less unusual means of dealing with actual or threatened interruptions of normal debt servicing. In some cases, commercial banks have been willing to conclude longer-term arrangements. There were 13 formal reschedulings for IMF–World Bank member countries in 1981, 10 in 1982, and 31 (involving twenty-one countries) in 1983. Although more than 30 reschedulings were negotiated in 1984, formal agreement was reached on only 21, involving sixteen countries and $11 billion of debt. More than $115 billion was under negotiation in 1984, four-fifths of which was accounted for by Argentina, Mexico, and Venezuela.[94]

Rescheduling negotiations have proceeded on a case-by-case basis. Generally, creditors have insisted that the debtor country have in place an upper credit tranche program with the IMF. Spreads over London Interbank Offer Rate (LIBOR) for interest rates on rescheduled debts are reported to have declined from a range of $1\frac{7}{8}$ to $2\frac{1}{2}$ percentage points in 1982 and 1983 to $1\frac{1}{8}$ to 2 percentage points in 1984. Rescheduling fees also declined in 1984 and, in some cases, were waived.[95]

The procedures followed until now have been successful in avoiding disruption of the international financial system, but the costs have been heavy for a number of debtor countries. The debtor countries as a group have achieved a great reduction in the current account deficit in their balance of payments, initially by reducing imports but later by expanding exports. However, per capita gross domestic product remains below previous levels in many countries. The situation of the major debtors has received the greatest public attention because of its implications for the international financial system. Very poor countries and some middle-income exporters of primary products may face less manageable problems.[96]

In June 1984 leaders of a number of Latin American countries called attention to the severity of the region's external debt problems and declared that responsibility for resolving them should be shared by creditor and debtor countries, the commercial banks, and multilateral lending agencies such as the IMF. At a meeting in February 1985, the economic and foreign ministers of the eleven most heavily indebted Latin American

94. Ibid., pp. xiv–xvii.
95. Ibid., p. xv.
96. Ibid., p. viii.

countries (the Cartageña group) reiterated their proposals for a new approach to the debt problem.[97] In April 1985 ministers of the Group of 24 on International Monetary Affairs called for "the establishment of special facilities in the International Monetary Fund to alleviate the burden of higher cost of debt through such mechanisms as an interest subsidy account and the enlargement of the compensatory financing facility by providing additional resources to alleviate debt servicing arising from increases in interest rates."[98]

Proposals for special debt relief facilities have not attracted the approval of industrial countries. Spokesmen for these countries have endorsed the case-by-case approach to debt problems and have stressed the importance of IMF-supported adjustment programs for debtors and of closer cooperation between the IMF and the IBRD.[99]

Despite the accomplishments of the existing procedures and the absence of an immediate crisis, it may be prudent for the international community to further consider establishing new arrangements to cope with the debt problem. The patience and commitment of lenders and borrowers and the political support of debtor countries may erode or may be damaged severely by an external shock. Failure of the adjustment programs or rescheduling negotiations of some major debtors, interruption of expansion of economic activity in industrial countries, or a sharp increase in real interest rates could revive the debt crisis. Institutionalized debt relief may be needed to deal with debt problems in a more certain and equitable way and, thus, help ensure the continued stability of the financial system, expanding trade, and an orderly flow of capital to developing countries on reasonable terms.

The term *debt relief* can cover a range of actions extending from rescheduling amortization payments at unchanged, or increased, interest rates to substantial forgiveness. Here, attention will be directed mainly to debt relief in the sense of a reduction in the present value of debtors' future obligations for payments of interest and principal. Such relief

97. Letter from the presidents of seven Latin American republics, reported in *New York Times*, June 7, 1984; communiqué of conference of economic and foreign ministers of eleven Latin American countries held in Cartageña, Colombia, June 21–22, 1984, summarized in *IMF Survey*, July 2, 1984, pp. 201–02; communiqué of meeting of the same group held in Santo Domingo, Dominican Republic, February 7–8, 1985, summarized in *IMF Survey*, February 18, 1985, p. 55.

98. *IMF Survey*, April 29, 1985, p. 134.

99. See, for example, communiqué of the heads of state or government of seven major industrial countries, published in *IMF Survey*, June 18, 1984, pp. 188–90; statement of Paul A. Volcker, chairman of the Board of Governors of the Federal Reserve System, before the House Committee on Foreign Affairs, 98 Cong. 2 sess. (August 8, 1984).

would require either that creditors give up some of their claims or that debtors receive official aid. If, however, debt relief lessened the risk of default, the risk-adjusted present value of creditors' claims would not necessarily be reduced and might be increased.

Debt relief could take the form of restructuring outstanding debt to provide longer maturities, lower interest rates, a limit on interest payments on floating-rate loans, some reduction of the principal, or a combination of these. Many combinations of maturities, interest rates, and principal amounts have equal present values and, in that sense, are financially equivalent for lenders and borrowers; however, differences in the timing of debt service payments and in accounting and bank regulatory treatment may be significant for both debtors and creditors. The choice of the exact combination could be open to negotiation.[100] An alternative to debt restructuring might be the establishment of an international program to help countries meet debt service payments resulting from increases in interest rates. Either of these forms of assistance to debtors might be accompanied by changes in procedures and policies with respect to debt rescheduling.

Economic arguments for debt relief are that debtors' efforts to meet existing debt service requirements may damage national and international prosperity or that their inability or unwillingness to make the full debt service payments may result in large-scale defaults, with harmful effects on international financial stability. A political or moral argument is that debt relief is justified because unforeseen economic changes have unfairly increased the burden on debtors. Creditors could be asked to bear a larger part of the costs associated with debt restructuring on the grounds that debt problems are due to overlending as well as to overborrowing. Another political argument is that the perception of unfairness or excessive pressure on debtors may cause political disruption and withdrawal of popular support for governments of certain debtor countries.

Debt relief would be most likely to be acceptable and successful if it could meet three conditions: first, if relief were extended selectively to countries that needed it most and that were willing to implement balance

100. For a general discussion, see Peter B. Kenen, "Debt Relief as Development Assistance," in Bhagwati, ed., *The New International Economic Order*, pp. 50–77, and Paul Streeten, "Comment," in ibid., pp. 78–80. Recent proposals are described and evaluated by William R. Cline, *International Debt: Systemic Risk and Policy Response* (Washington, D.C.: Institute for International Economics, 1984), pp. 130–49; and C. Fred Bergsten, William R. Cline, and John Williamson, *Bank Lending to Developing Countries: The Policy Alternatives*, Policy Analyses in International Economics 10 (Washington, D.C.: Institute for International Economics, 1985).

of payments adjustment programs enabling them to service the restructured debt; second, if the costs were shared on a basis widely deemed to be equitable; and third, if the future flow of financing to developing countries were not jeopardized.

Whether it would be possible to agree on the need for a debt relief facility and to devise a plan satisfying the three conditions is uncertain. If agreement could be reached on the general principles, there would be advantages in assigning the program to the IMF. The IMF is already deeply involved in debt rescheduling and, as mentioned earlier, an IMF-approved adjustment program is usually a prerequisite for rescheduling. In 1983 and 1984 the IMF appeared to be taking more initiative than in the past in proposing the provisions of rescheduling arrangements. The operation could be entrusted to a new legally separate entity attached to the IMF. This form of organization would avoid the need to amend the IMF's Articles of Agreement, a difficult and time-consuming process. The governing body, management, and staff could be the same as those of the IMF proper.

Different versions of a debt-relief operation can be visualized. The versions being considered here would extend the case-by-case approach that has been successfully followed until now. Presumably, however, a relief facility, though possibly authorized in advance, would come into operation only when there was broad agreement that a number of countries urgently needed debt relief.

A possible procedure would begin with the IMF proposing, after discussions with the interested parties, debt restructuring plans and accompanying adjustment programs for countries facing especially severe difficulties. Negotiations between the parties would follow. Relief could be provided by the commercial banks and other lenders exchanging their outstanding claims for new obligations with the appropriate combination of face amount, interest rate, and maturity. Some way would have to be found to induce participation by creditors holding the bulk of the outstanding debt.

One ambitious scheme would be to replace existing debt with a reduced amount of direct obligations of the new IMF affiliate, which would act as an intermediary receiving service payments from the debtor country and making payments to the creditors. Another arrangement, differing mainly in form, would be for the IMF affiliate to guarantee the obligations, which would justify lower interest rates. The amounts involved, however, could be very large. It might be more feasible to reach agreement on a plan providing guarantees only for increased lending by creditors that participated in granting relief for old debt.[101] Since the IMF affiliate would have no assets or credit of its own, its obligations or guarantees would have to be underwritten by the governments or central banks of participating industrial countries.

An alternative to the approach sketched in the preceding paragraphs would be to create a debt-relief entity attached jointly to the IMF and the World Bank rather than to the IMF alone. This would have the advantage of bringing to the operation the expertise of the Bank's staff and the Bank's access to market borrowing and cofinancing with other lenders. It would tend to emphasize the role of medium-term and long-term programs to strengthen debt-servicing capacity.

The gains from a successful debt-relief facility are potentially great but hard to demonstrate in a convincing way because of uncertainty about the magnitude of the risks that the facility could insure against. The staff of the IMF has concluded that the debt problem is manageable, without a relief facility, given sustained recovery in the industrial countries, appropriate adjustment policies on the part of debtor countries, and careful credit management by lenders.[102] Other studies have reached similar conclusions, with various degrees of confidence.[103] The risk of an unfavorable outcome, nevertheless, appears to be great enough to warrant further consideration of debt-relief proposals and contingency planning.[104]

A general debt-relief facility could not be justified primarily as aid to the poorest countries since the major borrowers include newly industrializing countries and oil exporters whose per capita incomes are higher than those of most developing countries. However, some of the poorest countries face severe external debt problems. Some creditor countries might be willing to offer poor countries partial forgiveness of official credits on a selective basis as a supplement to a debt-relief facility. The Federal Republic of Germany, for example, in 1978 adopted a policy of

101. On similar proposals, see Richard S. Dale and Richard P. Mattione, *Managing Global Debt* (Brookings, 1983), pp. 42–48.

102. IMF, *World Economic Outlook*, 1984, pp. 20–25; speech presented by J. de Larosière, in *IMF Survey*, February 18, 1985, pp. 50–55; IMF, *World Economic Outlook, 1985*, pp. 50–63.

103. See Cline, *International Debt,* and studies cited by Cline at pp. 169–75; World Bank, *World Debt Tables, 1984–85*.

104. Cline concludes that, although adoption of "sweeping debt reform measures" would be "counterproductive," contingency planning should be undertaken to prepare for an unfavorable outcome if it should materialize. *International Debt,* p. 69. Bergsten, Cline, and Williamson argue, however, that the funds needed to support concessional restructuring of the debt would be made available only in response to a crisis. *Bank Lending to Developing Countries,* pp. 85–86.

extending grants rather than soft loans to the least developed countries and has forgiven earlier official loans to twenty countries.

A possible disadvantage of a debt-relief facility is that its existence might make debtor countries less willing to undergo hardships to meet their obligations. In practice, the managers of the facility might find it difficult to limit relief to the most needy countries.

The likely effect of a debt-relief facility on the flow of resources to developing countries is an important consideration. A negative effect would occur to the extent that commercial banks no longer felt pressure to increase their loans in connection with debt reschedulings to protect themselves against defaults.[105] It is true that, once a debt-relief operation had been concluded, banks would be relieved of that particular form of pressure. Before that, however, the banks would face essentially the same kind of decision as they do now, that is, they would have to decide whether additional lending was advisable because it would protect them against the risk of having to write down the value of their old claims.

After a debt-relief operation had been concluded, new lending to the debtor country could become less risky because the reduction of old claims, together with the IMF-sponsored adjustment program, would strengthen the debtor's ability to service the loans. That would surely be the case if credible guarantees were offered for additional loans. Commercial banks might then be persuaded to accept narrower spreads between their interest rates on new loans and their cost of money. However, any attempt to require banks to extend new loans at interest rates below their cost of money would be almost certain to fail and to deter lending.

Another way of looking at the effect of debt relief on lending to developing countries focuses on lenders' general attitudes rather than explicit financial analysis. The argument is that lending would be deterred because the existence of a debt-relief program would cause debtors to take their obligations less seriously and would encourage repetition of debt restructuring in the future. This criticism is plausible, but it is hard to say how much weight should be given to it.

It would be difficult to reach agreement on contingency plans for a debt-relief facility. Creditors are understandably reluctant to contemplate writing down the value of their claims unless convinced that it is unavoid-

105. Cline stresses the importance of such "involuntary" lending and the probability that establishment of a debt-relief program would cause it to diminish. *International Debt,* pp. 71–79.

able. Many debtor governments would no doubt welcome the idea of a facility but would be inclined to bargain hard for liberal terms. Developing countries that have been prudent in borrowing and that do not face acute debt problems might lack enthusiasm for the proposal. Governments of industrial countries might hesitate to support a proposal that could be seen as a bailout for large banks, a reward for profligacy, and a dangerous precedent.

A more modest approach than that discussed in the preceding pages would be for the IMF to establish a special policy for lending countries money needed to meet part of their interest payments on external debt due either to a sharp increase in interest rates above the average of recent years or to an excess of market rates over some agreed maximum real rate (a market rate adjusted by a price index). Since Fund credit under existing facilities helps meet interest payments as well as other foreign payments, a special policy would be a formalization and extension of practice rather than a completely new departure. Presumably, it would allow larger credits for this purpose, and would adjust access promptly for changes in interest rates.

In a broad sense, the policy would resemble the compensatory financing facilities for export shortfalls and cereal import excesses. The analogy suggests a significant proviso: the policy for interest payments should be designed to meet only temporary increases of interest rates. To that end, the increase in rates required to make it operative should be set on the high side, compared with past experience.

Access to the special credits should be conditional on the existence of a balance of payments need and on the country's following policies designed to prevent a further unsustainable growth of external debt. For countries already having a standby arrangement or extended Fund facility, the policies in place presumably would satisfy the conditions in most cases. The IMF would need to exercise moral suasion to prevent lenders from widening spreads between their lending rates and their cost of funds and to obtain narrower spreads and lower fees for countries with good performance.

An advantage of the special policy would be that it could be put in place quickly to help cope with high interest rates if that should be judged advisable. A disadvantage would be that lending to meet excess interest payments would be a palliative rather than a fundamental attack on the debt problem, and would be especially vulnerable to criticism as a bailout for lenders.

## Conclusions

As detailed in earlier sections of this study, the IMF has served as a channel for multilateral economic assistance to developing countries in the past. If a substantial consensus in favor of doing so should be reached, additional economic assistance could be provided through the Fund. The use of the word "through" is significant. The real-resource counterpart of the financial assistance would come from other countries, mainly industrial countries and some oil-exporting countries but also from some developing countries. The governments of these countries could permit the transfer of real resources in exchange for claims against the IMF or an IMF affiliate (reserve tranche positions, loans, or special drawing rights); or, they could make voluntary contributions, accept lower remuneration on creditor positions in the IMF, agree to the use of Fund gold for the benefit of developing countries, or assume contingent liabilities by guaranteeing IMF obligations. Generally, the provision of real resources would entail an economic cost, but in some cases the goods and services supplied to recipients of assistance could be produced by fuller use of labor and capital that otherwise would have been idle.

The previous section examined four possible forms of additional economic assistance to developing countries through the IMF—a subsidy for IMF charges, a soft-loan facility, an SDR link, and an external debt-relief facility. All of these would be related to the Fund's responsibilities and previous activities. They could be regarded as further steps in an evolutionary process that has brought significant changes in attitudes toward the Fund and in Fund operations since the Bretton Woods Conference in 1944 and the commencement of Fund transactions in 1947. The possible new schemes have been viewed in this paper as supplements to existing forms of assistance through the IMF and from other sources rather than as replacements for assistance now provided. Inevitably, however, there would be some degree of rivalry between any new form of assistance and existing forms.

The conclusions reached here about a possible SDR link and a debt-relief facility can be stated briefly and will be presented before the comments on the other schemes. A distinctive characteristic of an SDR allocation is that it provides unconditional liquidity as distinguished from the conditional credit extended through the IMF's basic financing and special facilities. An SDR allocation in normal form or, to a greater extent, an allocation giving preferential amounts to low-income participants would be helpful to developing countries, but neither could serve as a major form of assistance to developing countries. With the higher SDR interest rate (in relation to market rates) now received by holders and paid by users, the advantages accruing to original recipients have been greatly reduced, though not eliminated. The maintenance of an SDR interest rate that is competitive with the rates of return on other reserve assets has correctly been judged as essential for the acceptability of the instrument and its success. Although it would be possible to subsidize the interest rate payable by low-income users of SDRs, the advantages of that form of assistance over other forms are not evident. The absence of conditionality for receipt of SDRs would mean that the assistance could not be used as an inducement or leverage for improved policies; the absence of monitoring of SDR use would mean that there would be no safeguard against wasteful use. These criticisms would not apply to a link taking the indirect form of allocations to the IMF's general department or to development finance institutions.

The main drawback to a link is that insistence on it could divert attention from more important matters. There is no evidence that the developed countries have become receptive to the idea. In the absence of a consensus, debate about a link could delay or block additional allocations of SDRs that may become desirable to meet an urgent need for additional liquidity.

In the absence of a link, a sizable SDR allocation might offer an opportunity to persuade industrial countries to make voluntary contributions for a soft-loan facility. As explained earlier, no immediate balance of payments burden would be involved; if further SDR allocations should be made regularly, contributors' interest costs on SDRs turned over to the soft-loan facility could be covered from their allocations.

If a debt-relief facility were to be established, it would be preferable to assign it to an entity attached to the IMF or to the IMF and the World Bank rather than to a wholly new and untried organization. Many technical features of a practical facility remain to be worked out. The need for such a facility is uncertain. Further study and discussion are desirable before either accepting or rejecting the idea. Meanwhile, consideration might be given to a special Fund policy allowing drawings to cover part of increases in real interest rates on external debt of developing countries.

A subsidy for IMF charges payable by low-income countries would be the least novel of the four schemes examined in this paper. It would be capable of quick introduction and simple operation, and could be financed on a limited scale from uncommitted resources flowing from repayments of trust fund loans. It would neither enlarge limits on access to Fund credit nor extend the repayment period.

An IMF soft-loan facility such as that outlined earlier would offer credit to low-income countries subject to the normal kind of Fund conditionality. But interest rates would be lower and the repayment period longer than for the Fund's basic financing and most of its special facilities, and perhaps longer than the outside limit of ten years for repayment of drawings under the extended facility. The purpose would be to help the recipients follow policies designed to eliminate unsustainable balance of payments deficits without imposing excessive hardships on them or unnecessarily depressing international trade.

In principle, the conditionality, though similar to that for other upper credit tranche standby arrangements, could be less severe because the low interest rates and longer repayment period would lessen and defer the balance of payments surplus that would have to be achieved to repay the Fund. In practice, the projections underlying adjustment programs might not be accurate enough to allow a fine calibration of the severity of conditions.

An objection likely to be raised against a proposal for an IMF soft-loan facility is that it would duplicate, or conflict with, World Bank lending. In weighing this argument, a distinction should be made between types of Bank loans. As explained earlier, the World Bank's project loans and most of its sector loans serve different purposes from those of IMF credits. These Bank loans (which comprise the bulk of the Bank's total lending) can be used only to pay for designated imports; furthermore, the recipient usually is required to make additional local-currency expenditures, which indirectly increases the demand for imports. The Fund's credits, in contrast, supply freely usable foreign exchange that enables a country to cover a balance of payments deficit due to causes unrelated to the Fund transaction. Any duplication or conflict would arise with respect to the World Bank's structural adjustment loans, which supply resources usable for all foreign payments except for a few specified purposes. In the five fiscal years ended June 30, 1980, through June 30, 1984, these loans constituted 6.8 percent of total IBRD loans and IDA credits.

A difference between the World Bank's structural adjustment loans and an IMF soft-loan facility of the kind under discussion is that the Bank's program has not been limited to loans to low-income countries at low interest rates. Structural adjustment loans have been made to relatively high-income and middle-income developing countries including Yugoslavia, Panama, Turkey, and Korea as well as to low-income countries like Malawi, Pakistan, Togo, and Kenya. Most structural adjustment loans have carried regular IBRD interest rates, but some have been granted on highly concessional (IDA) terms.

An institutional difference between the Bank's structural adjustment loans and Fund credit is that the Bank's loans appear to take much longer to draw up and usually seem to be disbursed more slowly.[106] For this reason and because rollovers or increases of commercial bank loans and debt rescheduling are often made contingent upon the existence of a Fund-supported program, Fund credit is better suited to help meet emergencies. These differences are related to differences in the purposes and operating styles of the two institutions.

Although there may be a fairly wide overlapping area in programs supported by the Bank's structural adjustment loans and Fund credits, there are significant differences in emphasis. Both institutions encourage countries to adopt pricing policies, interest rates, and fiscal incentives to improve the efficiency of resource use and, thus, to foster growth and strengthen the balance of payments. The Bank is especially concerned with institutional and organizational reforms and with investment programs, whereas the Fund is especially attentive to general financial measures and exchange rates and exchange and payments systems. The formal conditions for the Bank's structural adjustment loans appear to be more numerous and varied than the performance criteria for the Fund's upper tranche credits. These differences are related to the Articles of Agreement of the two institutions and to their experience and the expertise of their staffs. To avoid inconsistent or conflicting advice and conditions for credit, it is necessary to have continued cooperation between the Bank and the Fund, within the framework of an understanding about the special functions of each.

At the international political level, the World Bank seems to enjoy more harmonious relations than the Fund does with the governments of developing countries. The IMF has been charged with insisting on excessive austerity and being insensitive to the aspirations of developing countries. In the short run, the reputation of the IMF would not necessarily be a net disadvantage in connection with the establishment of a soft-loan

106. Structural adjustment loans are disbursed more quickly than project loans. Accelerated disbursement of structural adjustment loans and certain other loans in selected cases is part of the special action program adopted by the World Bank in 1983. *World Bank Annual Report, 1984*, pp. 47–48.

facility. Indeed, it might well be an advantage in the eyes of industrial countries and those developing countries that pursue prudent and orthodox policies. Over a period of years, the perception of the World Bank may change if structural adjustment lending on terms requiring politically difficult actions by borrowers becomes a larger fraction of Bank lending and a relatively more important source of general purpose finance for balance of payments deficits. As mentioned earlier, the ability of the Bank to avoid confrontations with member governments in the past may have been due largely to the multiplicity and relatively small size of its individual loans. Applications for project and sector loans can be delayed or refused without seeming to render an unfavorable judgment on the member country's broad policies and creditworthiness, but it may be harder to avoid such an implication if a structural adjustment loan is refused.

These considerations indicate that the World Bank's lending does not now perform—and is unlikely to perform in the future—the same functions as an IMF soft-loan facility.

Another set of issues relates to the broad question whether the establishment of an IMF soft-loan facility would detract from the Fund's ability to perform its other functions. A specific issue is whether a soft-loan facility would divert resources from other Fund operations. A limited facility could be financed from the Fund's existing ordinary resources, but a full facility would require additional resources from gold sales, contributions, or other sources. Even if financed from additional resources, the operation of a soft-loan facility could diminish the Fund's capacity to borrow for other purposes or to obtain quota increases. To put that risk in perspective, it may be noted that access to a facility such as that discussed in this paper would be limited to low-income countries holding a small fraction of total Fund quotas. For those countries, soft loans would be mixed with other IMF credits in varying proportions. The volume of soft loans would have to be adjusted to the available resources. Before a soft-loan facility could be established, the Fund staff would undoubtedly be required to carry out simulations of usage with alternative specifications and alternative economic scenarios. Such studies would furnish a basis for setting the initial terms for access, charges, and repayment period, and for modifying the terms in the light of experience.

More intangible, but possibly more important, is the influence that the creation of a soft-loan facility might exert on the attitudes of member governments. Would it cause officials and other influential persons in industrial countries to consider the IMF a development or aid institution rather than a monetary institution? Would it deter industrial countries from supporting the Fund and using its resources when appropriate?

That concern already exists about the Fund's orientation is suggested by a communiqué issued after a May 1984 meeting of ministers and central bank governors of the Group of Ten countries. The communiqué included the statement that "it was essential to maintain and safeguard the monetary character" of the IMF. Clues to the meaning attached to "monetary character" are offered by the further statements that the ministers and central bank governors "attached particular importance to the revolving nature of . . . [the Fund's] financing," which should be available "with appropriate conditionality to support balance of payments adjustment."[107]

The emphasis of the Group of Ten representatives on the revolving character of IMF financing suggests the advisability of caution in lengthening the repayment period for soft loans beyond the limit of ten years that has been set for the extended facility. Soft loans would be conditional and consistent with the insistence that IMF financing be intended to support balance of payments adjustment. In the past, lending at below-market rates of interest and explicit subsidies financed from sources other than the Fund's general resources have been regarded as consistent with the Fund's monetary character.

There is little reason to suppose that the existence of a soft-loan facility would in itself discourage industrial countries from using the Fund's resources. In recent years, these countries have not borrowed from the Fund because they have felt less need to support their exchange rates than they did in the past and because credit has been available to them from other sources. If and when these conditions change, some of the industrial countries may again turn to the Fund for large credits. Meanwhile, the Fund's principal functions will continue to be lending to developing countries, consultation with all members, and surveillance of exchange arrangements and international liquidity.

The attitude of developing countries toward the IMF tends to differ from that of the industrial countries. For example, communiqués issued after meetings of ministers of the Intergovernmental Group of 24 on International Monetary Affairs held in April 1984 and September 1984 called for a change in the balance between conditional and unconditional liquidity, to be effected by substantial annual allocations of SDRs and the establishment of a link between SDR allocations and development fi-

107. For the text of the communiqué, see *IMF Survey*, June 4, 1984, p. 168.

nance. The ministers favored "a thoroughgoing reform of the international monetary and financial system" to meet the special concerns of developing countries. They recommended convening an international monetary and financial conference for that purpose.[108]

The establishment of an IMF soft-loan facility might be welcomed by developing countries as a partial response to their concerns. It could help deflect demands for the radical restructuring of the IMF or its replacement, while enhancing the Fund's capacity to encourage balance of payments adjustment.

Whatever may be the merits of the proposals discussed in this paper, their advancement is less important for the industrial countries than are the present operations of the IMF. That is probably true also for the developing countries. Hence, priority should be given to supporting those operations with adequate resources from Fund quotas and borrowing.

108. For the texts of the communiqués, see *IMF Survey*, April 3, 1984, pp. 117–19; *IMF Survey*, October 15, 1984, pp. 294–97.